American Capitalism and the Changing Role of Government

Harry G. Shaffer

PRAEGER

Westport, Connecticut
London

Library of Congress Cataloging-in-Publication Data

Shaffer, Harry G.
   American capitalism and the changing role of government / Harry G.
Shaffer.
      p.   cm.
   Includes bibliographical references and index.
   ISBN 0–275–96578–3.—ISBN 0–275–96658–5 (pbk. : alk. paper)
   1. United States—Economic policy—1993–   2. United States—Social
policy—1993–   3. Capitalism—Moral and ethical aspects—United
States.   4. Free enterprise—Moral and ethical aspects—United
States.   I. Title.
HC106.82.S5   1999
338.973—dc21   98–56638

British Library Cataloguing in Publication Data is available.

Library of Congress Catalog Card Number: 98–56638
ISBN: 0–275–96578–3
      0–275–96658–5 (pbk.)

First published in 1999

Praeger Publishers, 88 Post Road West, Westport, CT 06881
An imprint of Greenwood Publishing Group, Inc.
www.praeger.com

Printed in the United States of America

The paper used in this book complies with the
Permanent Paper Standard issued by the National
Information Standards Organization (Z39.48–1984).

10 9 8 7 6 5 4 3 2 1

To my life's companion, my best friend, my wife, Betty; to my children, Bernie, Ron, Len, and Tanya; to my wife's children, René and Jamie; and to our grandchildren, Alex, Benjamin, Gabe, Jake, and Natalie. May they and their children and grandchildren question every conventional wisdom, no matter how loudly proclaimed, how often repeated, and how widely accepted, always with the public good first and foremost in their minds.

Contents

Acknowledgments

I want to take this opportunity to express my gratitude to those who were of such invaluable assistance in the preparations of the manuscript for this book: U.S. physician and lung specialist Dr. William F. Porter; Health Service Administration Professor at the University of Kansas Dr. Michael H. Fox; and Canadian physicians Drs. Ann and Simon Carette, who contributed ever so much to the chapter on Health Care; low-income housing specialist Martha Taylor, who was very helpful with the chapters on Social Security and Welfare; and Dr. Beatrice Wright, who read several chapters and made many poignant suggestions.

I owe special gratitude to those who took so much time from their work and personal obligations to go over the entire manuscript word by word, sentence by sentence, and page by page and found numerous imperfections, from spelling errors and deficiencies in grammar and sentence structure to statements that needed clarification, and who made innumerable valuable suggestions for additions, alterations, and improvements: economists and specialists in comparative economic and political systems Drs. Frank Durgin, Tom Karler, William Mandel, and the late Lynn Turgeon; and "intelligent non-economists" (for whom, after all, this book is written) Norma Lauring and my wife, Betty. Although I alone bear responsibility for the contents and for any remaining errors and shortcomings, the book could not have been what it is without their help. Last, but certainly not least, I must express my gratitude to Denny Brown who, busy as she was as administrative officer at the University of Kansas School of Journalism, always found time to type and retype, cheerfully and patiently, correction after correction and version after version of the manuscript, and in so many other ways played a major role in the preparation of the final draft. I don't know what I would have done without her.

Introduction

Capitalism, the free enterprise system under which we presumably live: What is it? What is its underlying philosophy? How is the free market, unfettered by outside interference, supposed to meet the peoples' needs and expectations? Does it, will it, CAN IT do so effectively and with a minimum of government regulation and constraints?

This book will take a careful look at questions such as these; will focus on such economic and social problems as poverty, unemployment and inflation, the national debt, education, health care, and environmental concerns; and will address some of our most widely held conventional wisdom.

Coined by the American economist and diplomat John Kenneth Galbraith (1908–), the term "conventional wisdom" refers to something almost everyone agrees is true and correct, except that it ain't necessarily so. During the Middle Ages, the conventional wisdom had it that the earth was flat and if you came to the end of it, you'd better watch out or you'd fall off; for centuries, the conventional wisdom in Japan held that the emperor derived his divine powers from God and that the one sure way to go straight to heaven was to die for the empire. During the feudal era, everyone knew that you were born into a certain class in society, be it as a slave, a serf, or a member of the aristocracy, because God had reserved that place and position on earth for you, and to try to rise in the social scale would be a deadly sin. Today, the conventional wisdom has it that a balanced budget is the height of economic sagacity and farsightedness, that the profit motive is an absolute necessity for the achievement of economic efficiency and growth, that low interest rates are an unmitigated blessing, that more jails and tougher sentencing are the answers to our drug problems, and that most adult welfare recipients and homeless could and should get jobs.

Many of today's widely held views remind me of the student who did poorly on a test and afterward said to his professor: "It ain't what I don't know what gets me in trouble; it's what I know for sure that ain't so." So you can expect this book to challenge much of today's "conventional wisdom" and try to dispel some widely believed myths.

But can you presume that I will be objective and unbiased in my presentation and analysis? Perhaps this question should be asked somewhat differently: Can social scientists (economists, political scientists, sociologists, etc.) be truly objective? They don't have it easy, to be sure; certainly not as easy as scientists in the physical sciences. The physicist, the chemist, or the meteorologist simply is not faced with the same problems as one who deals with economic, political, and social issues. Suppose that it is your task as an astronomer to measure as exactly as possible the distance from the earth to a certain star in another galaxy, or as a chemist to find a fertilizer that increases output without increasing soil toxicity. You have no preconceived ideas as to the right answers, no long-held prejudices, no personal stake in these issues other than solving the problem at hand.

But how different is this in the social sciences and especially in economics: Whether prices go up or down, whether taxes are raised or lowered, whether more money is spent on education or on improving our highway system, whether or not equal rights laws are enforced, gun control laws are enacted, or hospital nursing staffs are downsized—issues such as these affect each and every one of us personally. We find it difficult to look at them impartially; we tend to prejudge and arrive at foregone conclusions. How would you feel, for instance, if you read in the newspaper that tens of thousands of U.S. steelworkers walked out on strike, demanding higher wages and fringe benefits? Would you be willing to study the matter "objectively" before making up your mind, to compare these workers' wages with wages of workers in similar industries such as coal miners or cement workers, to check into the cost of living in the areas where these workers live as compared with those where the other workers live, to find out what has happened to price levels and to changes in productivity since the last wage increase, and to look into the profits of the companies involved (so as to see whether they *can* grant wage increases without going broke)? Not likely. In all probability, you'll be for or against the strike before you know much about it. If you come from a certain orientation, a certain school of thought, you might well feel that the workers should be grateful for what they have. All the companies are asking for is an honest day's work for what surely is an honest day's pay—probably the highest anywhere in the world. And it's the general public—all of us—who suffer from these strikes. The workers lose days, weeks, or even months of wages; the company's financial position becomes shakier; and costs of production go up (and therefore, so do prices for consumers). If those workers are that dissatisfied, why don't they go elsewhere, to some other country, and see how they like it there? But if you come from a different background, your way of thinking might be diametrically opposite. You may feel that these workers ought to get higher wages. They work hard, this is the richest country in the world, the wealthy have more than their fair share already, and who should share in our wealth if not our working people who, after all, create it?

Being objective in the social sciences is also much more difficult because of what has come to be known as "the tyranny of words." In the physical sciences, words have clearly defined meanings: a yard is a yard, an ounce is an ounce, a degree of temperature is a degree of temperature, and there is no dispute as to what these words mean. But what is freedom? What is democracy? What is justice? What is an adequate distribution of income? What is a fair wage? Moreover, it's not only that different words have different meanings to different individuals; it's also that the same thing can be expressed in different ways that convey a quite different impression. Taking a calculated risk seems a sensible endeavor; gambling (which *is* taking a calculated risk) may be objectionable to some people. Governmental assistance to farmers to save the family farm may seem reasonable; using taxpayers' money to further special interests may not. Isn't it awful if a president always waffles, but isn't it great if he is flexible? The American columnist Hal Boyle brilliantly illustrated this when, during the war against Japan, he described what American newspapers were saying and what they meant:

The enemy is fleeing in confusion means *they are running.*

We made a planned withdrawal to strengthen our positions means *we are running.*

A courageous charge in the face of bitter enemy resistance means *we are advancing.*

A suicidal attack by crazy oriental fanatics means *they are advancing.*

We captured two major railroad towns in a lightning assault means *we took two towns.*

We withdrew from two minor villages in order to straighten out our lines means *they took them back.*

We were forced by inclement weather to find secondary targets means *our bombs missed again.*

Under the circumstances, I cannot claim to be totally objective or totally unbiased because I do not believe that's possible in the realm of social sciences. But honesty dictates that I convey to the reader in advance some idea as to where I stand, where my priorities lie, and how I intend to treat the subject at hand.

To begin with, I cannot subscribe to traditional economic views which treat economics in isolation from other social sciences and tend to exaggerate the role of the individual, paying but scant attention to society as such. Especially when evaluating an entire economic and social system, I feel much more akin with modern-day socioeconomists who see economics as a broader field which, to be meaningful, must give due consideration to historical, political, social, psychological, and other aspects that influence a country's economy; and they refuse to dismiss society as an empty concept, signifying but an aggregation of "sovereign" individuals. However, the realization that economics must go beyond its focus on the individual is actually not all that new; it dawned on traditional economists long ago. In 1890, for instance, the renowned British economist Alfred Marshall (1842–1924) wrote, in his *Principles of Economics*:

Just as a cathedral is something more than the stones of which it is made, as a person is something more than a series of thoughts and feelings, so the life of society is something more than the sum of the lives of its individual members.

I will argue in this book that, important as the rights of individuals undeniably are, they must be balanced against the individuals' responsibilities toward their community and yes, toward their less fortunate fellow citizens also; and society in turn has responsibilities toward all its members. Hence, I cannot accept the widely prevalent view that the functions of government ought to be minimized. I rather tend to agree with the position taken by President Lyndon B. Johnson when he said, "Government is not an enemy of the people; it is the people themselves," and "If government is to serve any purpose, it is to do for others what they are unable to do for themselves."

An economics student, overwhelmed by econometrics, mathematical models, game theory, input-output analysis, and what have you once told me that she thought that economics was but common sense made difficult and that its greatest usefulness was to provide gainful employment for economists. Maybe so, but this book is not likely to evoke such impressions in anyone, for it will refrain from statistical and graphic analysis understandable only to the professional. Written for the intelligent lay reader and the beginning economics and political science student, it is intended to examine and look critically at our country's economic and social structure, policies, and problems. It may not have ready cures for all that ails us, but if it challenges the readers to question long and widely accepted beliefs and to expose themselves to a wide variety of views before forming their own opinions on any controversial subjects, it will have fulfilled its purpose.

American Capitalism
and the Changing Role
of Government

Chapter 1

Capitalism: What It Is and What It Isn't—Theory and Practice

Only under capitalism, so the conventional wisdom has it, can a nation's economy flourish, prosper, and grow. Only a capitalist, free-enterprise economy, guided by the profit motive, can instill in individuals the economic incentive necessary for sustained maximum performance and efficiency. It alone, if allowed to exert itself in freedom and without intervention, can heal all that ails our economy and lead us to lasting prosperity. Hence, the smaller the role of government and the less the government interferes, we are told, the better off the country will be.

To evaluate this proposition, let us first understand how in theory such a free enterprise system is supposed to function. Then, let us investigate whether in fact it can and does live up to its promises.

While some aspects of a free enterprise system were already in practical existence, the basic principles were first laid down in a book published in 1776 by the Scottish economist Adam Smith (1723–1790). Known as *The Wealth of Nations* (its full title was *An Inquiry into the Nature and Causes of the Wealth of Nations*), it has often been referred to as "the bible of capitalism" and it catapulted Smith into the ranks of the immortals. The 900-page treatise was written as a social and economic criticism of the then prevailing system of "mercantilism" under which absolute monarchs held absolute power and productive economic units, although mostly privately owned, operated under highly intrusive and restrictive economic controls and guidelines. In his magnum opus, Smith tried to answer the question that economists have tried to answer for countless generations: "What can be done to best advance the economic well-being of our nation?" And Smith's answer was: Just leave individuals alone, let them pursue their own self-interest; and if they are allowed to do so freely and without government meddling, they will automatically, as if guided by an "invisible hand," further the economic well-being of the nation. Here is how Adam Smith explains the basic philosophy of his "obvious and simple system of natural liberty."

Every man, as long as he does not violate the laws of justice, is left perfectly free to pursue his own interest his own way. . . . He intends only his own gain, yet he is . . . led by an invisible hand to promote an end which was no part of his intentions. By pursuing his own interest he frequently promotes that of the society more effectually than when he really intends to promote it . . . a principle so powerful, that it alone and without assistance is capable of carrying on the society to wealth and prosperity.

So in Smith's world, people will work or produce for you not out of the goodness of their hearts, not because they like you, not because they are ordered to do so, but simply because they deem it to be in their own self-interest. Yet, in this manner, your needs and the economic needs of society will presumably be met, automatically and without government guidance and control. In Smith's words:

It is not from the benevolence of the butcher, the brewer or the baker that we expect our dinner, but from their regard to their self-interest. We address ourselves, not to their humanity, but to their self-love, and never talk to them of our necessities, but of their advantage.

In such manner, Smith advocates the economic system now technically known as *laissez-faire* (let do), although Smith himself never used the term. (There is a tale that, long ago, at a time of war, the merchants of France gave their full financial support to their king. Once victorious, the king called the representatives of the merchants before him and asked them: "What do you want me to do, what edicts do you want me to pass, what rules and regulations do you want me to enact to reward you and your class, the merchants of France, for what you have done?" Whereupon, so the story goes, the merchants answered, "*laissez nous faire*," Let us do, leave us alone. Just don't lay down any edicts, rules, or regulations, and we'll be all right.) But how, one might ask, can the well-being of society be best advanced "automatically, as if guided by an 'invisible hand'," if everyone pursues only his or her own interest?

At first glance, the explanation would seem logical enough. What is the economic goal of society? Obviously, the production of goods and services. What kinds of goods and services? The goods and services that people want. Does it then take a government or a planning board to decide what goods and services should be produced? Not at all, a defender of a free enterprise system would argue. Individuals, guided by their own self-interest and their desire to maximize their income, will automatically produce the goods they can sell and offer the services people want. But suppose that a widely demanded commodity is in short supply, and so producers double and triple their prices. Should the government now step in to "protect" the consumer? "No," firmly assert the advocates of a "free market." Attracted by the higher prices, they assure us, competitors will enter the market, soon more of that commodity will be on the shelves, and competition among sellers will drive the price down. But suppose that under such competition the price drops so low that producers find it difficult to meet costs. Do we now need government to step in and decree minimum prices (below which no one is allowed to sell) or to subsidize producers? Not necessary, we are again assured. Should this happen, some producers will simply go out of business and the market will once more correct itself automatically. Which producers would go out of business, you might ask. Today, we would tend to say that the small producers would be the least likely to survive. But followers of Adam Smith would be unlikely to consider size the determining factor. It would be the least efficient, the highest-cost producers, they would contend, who would be eliminated in the competitive race, and that's as it should be.

Why then, if the system works so perfectly, so automatically, so efficiently, does it not exist anywhere in the world? Why do governments everywhere exert varying degrees of influence and control, subsidizing here, regulating, restraining, or prohibiting there? To begin with, even the most ardent protagonists of capitalism never conceived of it as a system without any economic role for government. There was a role, but it was to be limited, to be sure. "Anarchy plus a policeman," the nineteenth-century Scottish historian Thomas Carlyle (1795–1881) called it. And when Thomas Jefferson said that "the government that governs least governs best," he wasn't talking about a government that doesn't govern at all!

Adam Smith's *The Wealth of Nations* outlines basically three functions that government in his free society is called upon to perform:

First, the duty of protecting society from the violence and invasion of other independent societies; secondly, the duty of protecting, as far as possible, every member of the society from the injustice or oppression of every other member of it, or the duty of establishing an exact administration of justice; and, thirdly, the duty of erecting and maintaining certain public works and certain public institutions, which it can never be for the interest of any individual, or small number of individuals, to erect and maintain; because the profit could never repay the expense to any individual or small number of individuals, though it may frequently do much more than repay it to a great society.

All of us can surely agree with Adam Smith that national defense and the maintenance of law and order are proper functions for government, although we may not agree with one another as to what constitutes justifiable national defense and what laws should be on the books and should be enforced. Should we have gone into Vietnam? Should we have bombed Iraq in Operation Desert Storm in 1991 and in Operation Desert Fox in December 1998? Should we cut medicare but not military expenditures? Should marijuana be legalized? Should the death penalty be abolished? Questions such as these may be debatable. But surely no one would argue that the defense of one's home against an attack by a foreign power or, for that matter, by armed robbers, and the punishment of the perpetrators should be each individual's personal responsibility. This, obviously, must be a collective effort, organized and carried out by various levels of government.

But how about that third function Adam Smith assigned to government, namely, the production of essential goods and services that private industry wouldn't provide because it wouldn't be profitable? As examples, Adam Smith mentioned the paving and lighting of London's streets, the erection of playgrounds for children, and garbage removal (since the practice of poorer city dwellers of dumping garbage into the courtyards of their high-rise apartment buildings, rather than paying private garbage collectors, threatened their health and that of their neighbors.) Where should we draw the line today? Private real estate developers certainly cannot profitably build homes for people who can't afford to pay for them, nor can physicians earn a living providing medical services for the indigent. Yet, are adequate housing and health care not essential?

Beyond these three functions specifically reserved for government, Adam Smith and his immediate intellectual descendants, known as the early "classical" economists, made numerous exceptions to their general rule of "no government interference in the economy." Some were major exceptions: David Ricardo advocated the nationalization of the central bank and John Stuart Mill the nationalization of land. Even Adam Smith found economic tasks here and there that, he felt, government needed to perform. He wrote, for instance, in *The Wealth of Nations*, that it can get awfully cold in the winter in some parts of England, and if there is not enough coal, rather than to let the people freeze, the government should ship it there. But were we not led to believe that private entrepreneurs guided by the profit motive would take care of that "automatically"? So interested did I, the author, become in this issue that I decided to write my Ph.D. dissertation on it. I entitled it "The Economic Functions of Government in Early English Classical Economic Thought," and I went carefully through all the writings of the six best known early classical economists—Adam Smith, David Ricardo, Thomas Robert Malthus, Jeremy Bentham, James Mill, and his better-known son, John Stuart Mill—and in 388 pages I listed, classified, categorized, and documented all the exceptions these early protagonists of capitalism made to their general rule of laissez-faire. It soon became evident to me that if a nation were to incorporate a major part of these "exceptions" into its economic system, it would not truly be a free enterprise system; it would be a welfare state.

The early classical economists began to realize it; their followers, the neoclassical economists, became even more aware of it; and today we certainly know or should know that, for a number of reasons, Adam Smith's system of "natural liberty" never did, never will, and never could function as its original, fundamental theory intended. So let us now take a look at some of the reasons why an unfettered free market would often yield results very different from what we expected from its underlying philosophy, and very different also from what we want for our society—reasons that have made it imperative for governments the world over to intervene in a variety of ways in their countries' "free enterprise" system.

In Adam Smith's world, the consumer was to be the true sovereign, the ruler who would decide what is to be produced, by means of what, in America, has come to be known as "dollar voting." In other words, consumers simply cast their votes on the market by buying or not buying goods and services offered; the producers simply follow these commands, and consumers' well-being is assured. So what's wrong with that? Well, for a start, we have to realize that this system is not a democratic system. It's not one consumer, one vote, it's one dollar, one vote, and some consumers have very many votes on the marketplace, while others have very few. Hence, all too often luxury goods are produced for the few while the many lack basic necessities. To illustrate, assume for a moment that you have some money to invest and that you realize that, because of capital shortages and substantially greater risks, returns are likely to be higher in less developed countries than in the United States. You are willing to take a chance, and so you go to one of the less developed capitalist or semi-capitalist countries in Asia, Africa, or Latin America to find out what is needed there. It doesn't take you long to arrive at an answer: undernourished children everywhere clearly indicate a desperate need for milk. Are you now going to buy some grazing land and import dairy cows? Probably not, because if the people had enough money to buy milk at a price that would allow a reasonable return to investors, there would be dairy farms there. So you look around for more promising investment opportunities and you soon discover that in that country in which the majority of people go hungry most nights, 2 or 3 percent of the population are very wealthy and they have acquired a taste for French champagne. And so you start importing champagne, and soon you develop a flourishing business in that poverty-stricken land that could benefit so greatly from very different investments.

This, unfortunately, is not just a theory. This is the reality in much of the less developed world, where a more or less free-enterprise economy prevails and luxury for the few—extreme even by American standards—coexists with unbelievable poverty for the masses. Situations are usually even worse where maldistribution of wealth and income is exacerbated by right-wing, usually military, dictatorships. They may allow a relatively free market, but in practice it benefits primarily the few, while access to decent housing, education, health care, and job and business opportunities is scant for the underprivileged masses. On the other hand, in formerly less developed countries such as Japan and South Korea, who made great, steady economic progress for several decades (although experiencing serious economic slumps in the 1990s; see page 37), somewhat less self-serving governments assumed major roles in the economy as planners, regulators, and as instigators and providers of social services. Credit for economic evolution in the communist and formerly communist countries in the East can certainly not go to a free market; how, if laissez-faire were the answer, would one otherwise explain the economic success of China and Vietnam, where free enterprise is very limited and under strict central control (average per capita growth rates of over 6 percent for Vietnam and 8 percent for China for the decade from 1985 to 1995 although both of these countries were also affected by the overall Asian economic crises of the late 1990s), and the disappointing performances in Russia and in the formerly socialist countries of Eastern Europe that have become so much more free-enterprise-oriented? (Realizing that privatization and market control have gone too far and are not the answer to Russia's economic problems, Russian prime minister Yevgeny M. Primakov announced in December 1998 a Russian kind of New Deal to cope with economic disintegration. "What I have in mind," he said, "is not a totally regulated and planned economy but necessary state intervention in economic life.")

Even in a highly developed, wealthy country such as the United States, there are millions of inhabitants—not only the unemployed, the disabled, and the homeless, but also the many who work hard for minimum wages—who on their own do not have adequate votes on the marketplace to purchase decent housing or even minimum health care and who, without government assistance, would be desperately destitute. (More on this in subsequent chapters on "Distribution of Wealth and Income," "Welfare," etc.) And how about the vast majority of Americans, the broad middle classes to which most of us belong? Are we the living embodiment of what classical economists mean when they talk about "consumer sovereignty?" Do we as consumers freely and on our own know and choose what we want? Can we possibly know what's good for us so that we can dispense with government "intervention?" Hardly, although we'd like to think we do. Even those of us who have enough dollars to cast significant votes in the marketplace are actually guided and often misguided by advertisements from multibillion-dollar corporations who have learned long ago that a dollar spent on advertising yields more in profits than a dollar spent on product improvement. And they also know that for advertising to be successful it need not be informative; it doesn't even have to be truthful. Prospective customers are not swayed by logic or detailed analysis. Good advertising merely needs to be repetitive and appeal not so much to the intellect as to feelings and emotions. "Drink Coca-Cola," "Drink Coca-Cola," "Drink Coca-Cola," has been one of the most successful advertisements in American history. Do you ever ask for a Pepsi Cola or a Royal Crown Cola when you go to a restaurant? Even today, most people still don't; they ask for a coke. And if you do, are you sure that you like Coca-Cola best, or have you merely succumbed to the "Drink Coca-Cola" message? Surely, the producers of Coca-Cola never told you on their own how much sugar there is in a "classic" coke, or whether the caffeine in it is good for children. Similarly, from the producers of truly incredible numbers of cereals, you hear that their product is "new," "improved," "enriched," "light," "toasted," "exploded," or what have you, but have they ever told you by themselves, without government dictates, how much saturated fat there is in each helping, how much cholesterol, how many calories? Cigarette manufacturers do not debate, nor even mention, lung cancer. Instead, they'll show you a picture of a beautiful young woman, strolling along a sunny beach smoking "slims," or of a handsome young man on a horse, happily puffing away. And if that isn't enough, they'll readily supply you with other "valuable" information: They'll tell you over and over that "Lucky Strike means fine tobacco" (don't they all), that their cigarette is made with "toasted tobacco" (is toasted tobacco better for you? Anyhow, how does one toast tobacco?), or that theirs is the cigarette with the "micronite filter, the same filter that is used in our atomic energy laboratories." (Great! Now you know, at least, that the cigarette is not likely to blow up in your face.) Honestly, don't you think that the free market needs a "policeman," a government to inspect meat processing plants, to test medicines for possible toxic effects, to warn of the undeniable, detrimental effects of smoking, to stop the promotion of tobacco products aimed at the young, or to check on the safety of children's toys? Would you really want to leave it up to individual entrepreneurs, guided by the profit motive, to give honest information to consumers? How can one deny that there is a role for government, and a vital role at that, in the area of consumer information and protection? And don't you think brain surgeons need to be properly licensed before they operate on patients, and pilots properly trained and tested before they are allowed to fly passenger planes?

Next, as we have seen, the theory of laissez-faire promotes the concept of an identification of self-interest with the interests of the nation: just let's all pursue our own interests, and we'll automatically do what's best for society as a whole, so the theory says. But is that necessarily so? Was Charles E. Wilson, former secretary of defense in the Eisenhower administration, right when he said, "What's good for General Motors is good for the country"? Couldn't you think of numerous eventualities that would be good for General Motors but not for the rest of us? Wouldn't it be good for General Motors if Ford and Chrysler went out of business? Or if Toyotas, Nissans, and Mazdas were kept out of this country? Or if cars in general didn't last as long as they do? Or if we got involved in a little war so that GM could sell more jeeps and tanks to our armed forces? But would all that be what we would want for our country? Would it not be marvelous if we could live out our lives in perfect health, without ever getting sick? But would that be in the best economic interest of physicians, nurses, hospital administrators, or of our pharmaceutical industry? Wouldn't it be wonderful if we could eliminate all crime, if we never needed to lock our houses or cars nor fear walking the streets at nights? But what would that do to job opportunities for police officers, lawyers, judges, and jail keepers? No indeed, the identification of self-interest with the interest of society is not a valid premise. It's a myth, and no country could allow the self-interest of individuals and of corporate units to exert itself without supervision and restraints. After all, to give just one more example, would you want your next door neighbors in a residential area to keep dirty and badly smelling pigs in their backyard if they found it in their interest to do so, or do you approve of appropriate zoning restrictions?

By now, it should be evident that the entire laissez-faire philosophy stands and falls with the concept of freedom of competition. Free competition is the alpha and the omega, the beginning and the end; without it, the entire theoretical framework comes apart. Free competition is the sole tool, the only device that assures that the "right" goods be produced; it alone prevents sellers from charging unreasonable prices or from offering inferior goods; and it is the solitary guarantor of maximum efficiency since firms must be low-cost operators to survive in a competitive playing field. But in our society, competition exists only on the fringes of our economic system. There is still competition in the home service sector (plumbers, electricians, kids willing to mow lawns or shovel snow from driveways, for example). One can also still find significant competition among retail outlets and in agriculture, although giant department stores, chains, and supermarkets in the former and the rapid disappearance of family farms and their replacement by large, absentee-owned corporations in the latter have greatly reduced effective competition in those areas too.

In most industries—whether steel, automobile tires, or candy bars—the two, three, or four leading companies control the lion's share of the market. If free to do so, they could easily eliminate competition by agreeing on pricing, splitting territories (we will not sell in California if you don't sell in New York) or what have you, and have indeed often attempted to do just that in the past. Once again, government is called upon to intervene, in this case by setting and enforcing the rules of the game. So, under our antitrust laws, some of them dating back 75 or 100 years and more (such as the Sherman Antitrust Act of 1890 or the Clayton Act of 1914), attempts to effectively eliminate competition in interstate business activities are illegal; unfortunately, under pressure by special interest groups, these laws are all too often insufficiently enforced.

The entire problem of the lack of competition is greatly compounded by the presence of so-called "natural monopolies." Derived from the two Greek words *mono* (single) and *polein* (to sell), we talk about a monopoly when one single economic unit has exclusive control of a commodity or service in a given market. We refer to an industry as a *natural* monopoly when by its very nature it is ill suited for competition and operates much more efficiently without it. Take, for instance, electric light and gas, quite adequately supplied by single companies in most of our country. What would happen if we opened the market for these industries to competition? Each new electric company trying to compete with the existing one would have to erect new poles and connect new wires across the land, and each new gas company would need to tear up the streets and lay new pipelines where the old ones were entirely adequate to meet demand. What a senseless misuse of labor, raw materials, and capital! Free competition in such industries would clearly be unbelievably wasteful; but on the other hand, monopolists allowed to operate freely would surely find it to their advantage to force unreasonably high prices on the consumer.

Such being the case, don't we need government to superintend such "public utilities?" In our country, various levels of government—federal, state, or local government, as the case may be—do and obviously must restrict harmful competition in such natural monopoly industries (an exception to our antitrust laws) and then set "reasonable" prices, which we interpret to mean prices low enough so as not to exploit the consumer, yet high enough for a reasonable return to the investors—a task at the federal level assigned, for instance, to the Federal Trade Commission and the Federal Communications Commission for interstate and international transactions. The free market is certainly not equipped to deal with such problems by itself. In some instances, one should add, competition is not only undesirable but virtually impossible. Suppose there is a town satisfactorily supplied with water from a nearby source; but competitors would have to haul or pipe water in from 175 miles away—obviously not feasible from an economic point of view. What now? Should a private company be permitted to charge whatever the market would bear, even if it meant that people could no longer afford to water their lawns or wash their cars? The answer is evident: either government ownership and operation or our present way, government supervision and control.

Next, goods are produced and services rendered, but are they apportioned equitably in free-enterprise societies? Of course, what is "equitable" is a value judgment, a matter of opinion, and you and I might not agree on what constitutes an "equitable" distribution of income. In any case, how, in laissez-faire theory, is income supposed to be distributed? Surely not equally (that's equalitarian socialism), nor according to needs (that's perfect communism). No, in the theory of a free-enterprise economy, individuals are to be rewarded according to their contribution to the production of goods and services, and thereby to the well-being of society. But does it actually work like that? How does one assess an individual's contribution to the economic well-being of society? The market seems a biased judge, for it isn't the great teacher, the great scientist, or even the great political leader who is rewarded with extremely high incomes (even the president's salary is only a relatively small $200,000 per year). Apart from individuals with some unique abilities, such as great singers, performers, boxers, or baseball players, there is but one particular ability that is rewarded with extremely high incomes: business ability, and especially the ability to know when to buy and when to sell stocks on the stock exchange and to have enough money to do so on a grand scale. If I were to think of someone who made an outstanding contribution to the well-being of our society, it wouldn't be the president of the Chrysler Corporation or the owner of a casino in Las Vegas, and surely not the successful stock speculator. It would be someone like Dr. Salk who, with his invention of the Salk vaccine, virtually single-handedly wiped out infantile paralysis, that horrible disease that each year crippled tens of thousand of American youngsters and had parents in a frenzy for months on end during polio season. Dr. Salk did get respectable research grants and salaries, I am sure; but the millions and millions of dollars were made by the company that produced and sold the Salk vaccine. So, can we really say that the advertising manager of a major tobacco company contributes more to the general economic welfare of our country than a research physician who finds a cure for one of our fatal or crippling diseases? The market says so, but do you?

Anyhow, it isn't necessarily hard or efficient work that brings high

income since one can "contribute to production" by simply owning productive property or by letting others use one's land, one's capital, or
one's inherited or accumulated wealth; indeed, rent, interest, and profits
make up roughly one-third of our entire national income, a third that
goes mostly to but a small percentage of our population. As a matter of
fact, most of the upper 2 percent of income earners in the United States
derive only a very small part of their earnings from payment for work
performed.

A lack of economic security is a necessary by-product, a side effect, of
capitalism. A totally laissez-faire economy cannot offer its citizens any
assurance of even a minimum income. True, in none of the industrialized
countries are the old, the sick, the disabled, the unemployed left to shift
for themselves. But to the extent to which a government does provide
aid and assistance, to the extent to which those who have are made to
contribute to the well-being of those who have not, to that extent the
country has deviated from the philosophy of a free market in which
individuals are to be left alone to provide for themselves. And, as we
shall see in subsequent chapters, the United States stands rather low on
the totem pole, as far as governmentally provided social welfare measures are concerned.

Then, there are certain goods and services, such as railroad-crossing
barriers or lighthouses beaming guiding lights to ships at sea, that everyone can use simultaneously: no one can or wants to buy them for oneself,
and if you use them, you don't deprive others from using them also.
National defense would fall into this category; the soldiers who defend
you from enemy attack defend me also, whether I pay for it or not. Nor
can I easily, or would I want to purchase my own tornado warning
system. The siren that warns one warns all. Hence, the free market could
not and would not provide for it. Financing such "public goods" by
voluntary, private contributions would not be fair nor work satisfactorily
since the "bad guys," the free riders who did not contribute anything,
would enjoy the same military protection and tornado warning as the
"good guys" who did so willingly. Nor can people buy their own street
stoplights or hire a private company to remove snow along the city
streets between their home and work place, for I could then, without
paying, drive just as safely to work as they do. These kinds of "public
goods" must be and are provided everywhere by the public sector, by
some level of government, in other words, paid for out of taxes, and the
role of the private sector in these areas is necessarily minimal (private
bodyguards, private access roads to the home, and the like). To what
extent such services as education and health care should fall into the
publicly-provided-for-all, not-for-sale category is a much debated issue.

In our country, public policies have in recent years shifted back from
Roosevelt's New Deal and Johnson's Great Society to ever greater em-

phasis on the private sector. So we have today some 150 million passenger cars plus some 50 million trucks and buses but many of our roads and bridges are badly in need of repair. You find an almost unbelievable and ever-increasing assortment of consumer goods in all categories, but money for the protection of the environment is hard to come by, and expenditures for public education and public health dollars for the needy have failed in recent years to keep up with rising prices and increasing population and are under constant threat of further drastic cuts.

Throughout history, all capitalist economies have been plagued by the recurrence of economic recessions and depressions, involving massive unemployment and widespread suffering. Deemed periods of "necessary adjustments" by advocates of the free enterprise system, our government has, over the years, taken steps that have often mitigated them but have never succeeded in preventing their recurrence, a topic covered in greater detail in Chapter 3.

The defenders of orthodox capitalism assert that its greatest and most important economic advantage is maximum efficiency leading to maximum output of goods and services. But let us investigate first whether the market is really as efficient as it is alleged to be and, second, whether maximum efficiency ought to be a nation's primary goal.

For a starter, economic efficiency in laissez-faire economies rests on the assumption of what economists call "mobility of labor." In other words, workers, responsive to market forces, would readily move, not only from place to place but also from job to job and from vocation to vocation. Say, for instance, that at any one time there were too many tailors and not enough shoemakers. Compelled by competition, tailors would have little choice but to lower their prices, while shoemakers, in short supply, would be able to raise theirs. Consequently, so the theory goes, tailors would now shift from making clothing to making and repairing shoes. Great idea, but unfortunately, tailors don't know how to make shoes nor are their sewing machines equipped to attach soles and heels to the upper parts of boots. To some limited degree, this kind of mobility holds true for unskilled workers who might not be able to move readily from New Jersey to Florida, but could perhaps change from dishwashing to janitorial jobs. However, the more highly skilled, the more extensively trained workers are, the more difficult they will find it to shift. Chemists might discover that dentists currently earn more than they do, French teachers that they would be much better off teaching corporation law, but usually it's too late to start all over again. Without a central, overall plan, the market can make necessary adjustments only in the long run; future generations of college students may decide to go into the more promising, more remunerative careers—soon to discover, however, that so many have chosen the same road that by the time they graduate, theirs may no longer be the high-paying profession.

Capitalism has often been charged with promoting costly and ineffi-cient "anarchy of production." Indeed, in the absence of overall plan-ning, the system necessarily operates by trial and error. A Chinese restaurant locates in a town that doesn't have one. If it fails, too bad. If it's successful, soon a second, a third, a fourth open up and compete until it becomes clear that not all of them can make it. As a matter of fact, among newly opened small retail establishments, only one in three survives three years, and only one in ten a decade.

Inherent in the free market system is a certain type of waste of eco-nomic resources (land, labor, capital) that stems from an unnecessary duplication of efforts. Say, for example that there is a beach two miles long, and there is an obvious need there for a fast food stand. If you were a capitalist entrepreneur, intent on maximizing your profits, where would you locate such a place of business? Obviously, in the middle. If you were a planner in a socialist society, charged with setting up such a store for the maximum convenience of the customers, where would you locate it? Obviously, also in the middle. But look what happens when competition sets in. Suppose the planning authorities in the so-cialist society decide that the beach is too long and too crowded for just one such fast food establishment, where would they place two? To max-imize convenience and therefore efficiency of resource utilization, each should be half a mile from the end so that no one, no matter where on the beach, would have to walk more than half a mile to get to one of the two. But now suppose you were an entrepreneur in a market society, you wanted to open up such a beach front store, and there was already one there, right in the middle of the beach. Where would you put yours to maximize your profit potential? Obviously, not half a mile from one end, for that would leave the lion's share of the beach to your competitor. No, strangely enough, the best prospect would be right next to the ex-isting one. And if you both did well, where would a third one locate to compete? Most probably right next to the original one, on the other side. Inefficient and obviously wasteful as this may be, from the entrepre-neur's vantage point it makes sense. So don't be surprised when you find a McDonald's, a Wendy's, a Kentucky Fried Chicken, and half a dozen other fast food restaurants all on the same street within a couple of blocks from one another, as you probably will in most small American towns.

Of course, any economic system has certain built-in inefficiencies, and after all has been said, and if you measure efficiency of labor in terms of output per hour of labor time as Western economists do (ignoring such hidden costs as unemployment, erosion of the land, pollution of air and water, and squandering of often irreplaceable resources), market so-cieties have been doing rather well. But are defenders of orthodox cap-italism right when they tout maximum efficiency as the most important economic goal and when they assert that the resulting maximum output of goods and services will be like a rising tide that lifts all the boats? Unfortunately, this is not necessarily so. A high tide does nothing for the boats that are not in the water; and while it may well provide great sailing for the yachts and luxury liners, it often endangers and even sinks the small rowboats.

The author of this book will take the position that maximizing efficiency, desirable as it may be, should not necessarily be the primary objective when it comes into conflict with other social goals. After all, our system of justice is utterly inefficient. Maximum efficiency would demand that we arrest the suspect in the morning, try him in the afternoon and shoot him at night. Is that what we would want? From an economic point of view, it is hardly efficient to support the elderly who no longer contribute to the output of goods and services. Any suggestion on how to improve "efficiency" in that area? Increasing efficiency at the cost of neglecting environmental concerns, widening income inequality, or failing to address other social objectives may well be too high a price to pay.

Indeed, our society has many social goals to which the great majority of us subscribe; social goals which an unfettered free market has never achieved and by its very nature never will and never can achieve; goals such as sustained full employment, avoidance of the recurrence of depressions, quality education for all, protection of the public from unsafe products and services, equal rights for all irrespective of sex, race, creed, color, religion and, many would add, country of origin and even sexual orientation. Could you imagine living in a pure laissez-faire economy in which the old, the sick, the handicapped, the poor and hungry would be left to shift for themselves, and where the children of those who couldn't afford to pay would be left without schooling or medical care? Modern society could not possibly operate in such manner and survive in peace and prosperity. No indeed, except for the few anarchists among us, it's not a question of government versus no government; it's rather a question of how much government, for what purposes, and where the line should be drawn and the limits set. In answer to questions such as these, this book, this author will take the stand that President Franklin Delano Roosevelt took when he said that he "would rather have a government that errs on the side of compassion than a government frozen in the ice of indifference."

Chapter 2

Correct Economic Policy? What's Good for the Goose Is Not Necessarily Good for the Gander

When we are sick, we see a doctor who examines us, makes his diagnosis, and prescribes remedies. When we have a legal problem, we consult a lawyer who advises us and handles our case for us. But when it comes to our society's ills it's a different matter. There, we each have all the answers—although we are likely to change our opinions from time to time as we follow one or another group of "experts." You see, the problem is that these experts, these savants, these economic, political, and social gurus—our social scientists, analysts, columnists, commentators, talk show hosts, and political leaders—are in total disagreement with one another, not only as to antidotes and cures for maladies but often also as to what it is that ails us and that needs to be looked after and ministered to. And no wonder, because in this arena, what is good for the goose is not necessarily good for the gander. In the words of the Swiss psychologist Carl Gustow Jung, "the shoe that fits one person pinches another."

Take interest rates, for instance. Isn't it great that they have come down to much more reasonable levels since the early 1980s? It certainly helps if you want to buy a house or a car, and many homeowners have refinanced their mortgages at much more favorable rates. And it also makes it cheaper for businesses or government to float loans. But on the other hand, there are millions of people who have savings accounts, invest regularly in money market certificates, or in some other manner derive income from interest, and declining interest rates are the last thing they'd want to see. For some of them whose income consists primarily of interest and who could barely manage with the 12 percent returns we had in the 1980s, the current rates spell real hardship.

When, a few years ago, our country's currency was high in international markets, you could get a lot of German marks, French francs, or Japanese yen for your dollar. This made travel abroad cheap for American tourists and reduced the cost of Dutch cheese, Italian wine, or Mexican leather jackets to American consumers. Our domestic producers of such products were obviously less elated by the increased foreign competition; and our exporters were equally unhappy because foreign buyers found American products expensive, since they had to purchase the necessary dollars at highly unfavorable exchange rates. Under the circumstances, our international balance of trade became increasingly more negative, with imports exceeding exports by $10 billion a month and more. No wonder that our government, with the aid of friends and allies abroad, undertook steps to remedy the situation. In early 1993, we succeeded in lowering the value of the dollar by 35 percent and more against European currencies, and by mid-May of that year it reached a post–World War II low against the Japanese yen. All this surely helped domestic producers and exporters; but if you tried to buy a Volkswagen or a Toyota, you quickly discovered that you had to pay considerably more for it than you would have the year before; and vacations in Europe were no longer the bargain they used to be. (By 1998, when the dollar had once more risen significantly against the German mark or the French franc, the situation was temporarily reversed again.)

When oil prices dropped from a high of almost $40 per barrel in the early 1980s to $10 by July of 1986 (largely a result of Saudi Arabia's efforts to discourage domestic American energy production), manufacturers who use large quantities of oil found it easier to meet costs and operate profitably. And with gas prices at the pump as much as 20 to 30 percent and more below the level of the preceding year, all of us could drive our cars more economically. But good for everyone? All you had to do was ask around in Texas and other oil producing regions in our country. Owners of oil wells who had gotten rich at $30 and $40 a barrel started going bankrupt at $15, and if the domino theory applies anywhere, it seems to be at work here. Manufacturers who succeeded in selling oil drilling equipment to companies willing to borrow money for it at 15, 16, and 17 percent interest and more found that their sales had hit rock bottom, and that several of their regional outlets had gone out of business. Banks who had extended loans to oil drilling companies which, so it seemed then, could do no wrong were losing money and going broke. For every one dollar drop in oil prices, 25,000 workers in Texas lost their jobs and state revenues decreased by a $100 million in one year. What was true for the Lone Star State held similarly for Alaska, Oklahoma, Kansas, and other oil producing regions in our country. And the effects were even more devastating for such oil exporting countries as Mexico or the Soviet Union. But by the mid-1990s new technology had drastically lowered oil drilling and extraction costs in a number of countries. U.S. companies, for instance, now found it worth their while to explore beneath formerly impenetrable sheets of salt in the Gulf of Mexico—even at oil prices of $13 a barrel. So, did everyone benefit from that technological progress? Unfortunately not. Spurred on by skyrocketing oil prices in the early 1980s, investors had turned to alternate energies which proved able to furnish energy at costs of $20 to $25 per barrel of oil equivalent. Obviously, their investments quickly went sour when oil could be produced profitably at lower costs.

But there must be some economic state of affairs, some economic trend, some economic policy that would be beneficial to one and all. Take inflation, for instance. A really bad inflation surely hurts everyone while low rates of inflation or steady price levels must be good for all concerned. Not so, I am afraid. There is at least one group in society, namely, people who owe money, who benefit from rapidly rising price levels. Take a farmer who, greatly overextended in his debt obligations and with farm products down in price, finds it difficult to meet his monthly payments. With wheat at, let us say, $2.50 a bushel, he would have to sell 40,000 bushels to pay off a $100,000 debt. But if prices overall were to rise by 200 or 300 percent per year, as they did not long ago in Argentina, Brazil, and Israel, then, over a two- or three-year period, the price of wheat may be up to $10 or even $20 a bushel. Of course, the farmer's costs would go up also; but his $100,000 debt would not change. At $20 per bushel, he would need to sell only 5,000 instead of 40,000 bushels to pay off his loan. And if inflation continued at those rates for a few years, you might be able to pay off a substantial mortgage on your home with a month's wages or less.

Well, how about times of general prosperity, higher wages, higher profits, and higher consumer purchases? That can't be bad for anyone, can it? If you think it can't, just ask pawn brokers, owners of shoe repair shops, or bankruptcy lawyers. They all prosper during periods of economic depressions.

What it all amounts to, then, is this. It is virtually impossible for the government to come up with economic policies that would benefit all; and at times, attempts to please everybody border on the ridiculous. This, for instance, is the case when our government prohibits cigarette manufacturers from advertising on television, decrees that health warnings must be placed on each package sold, and puts a high tax on cigarettes to discourage smoking, especially by teenagers, while at the same time subsidizing tobacco growers, thus making it more profitable for them to produce the crop.

Under the circumstances, economic policy decisions become political decisions. Whom do we want to favor, whose interests should get priority attention? Should we promote the welfare of the poor at the expense of the general taxpayer? Should we adopt policies that help exporters at the expense of consumers? Should we pay farmers to take land out of production, although this leads to unemployment in the agricultural sector and to higher food prices for all of us? More often than not, there are no "right" or "wrong" answers. You have your preferences, your priorities, and I have mine. In the final analysis, what matters the most is who can exert the greatest influence in the legislative, administrative, and executive halls in Washington and in the state capitals. But unfortunately, those whose needs tend to be the most precarious— the children, the sick, the poor, the disadvantaged—are all too often the ones least able to make their voices heard. It then becomes morally imperative for others, better equipped to do so, to speak for them and to plead their case.

Chapter 3

Boom and Bust:
The Capitalist Experience

Capitalism, as an economic system, has been indicted on many counts, but none of these charges has been more clearly documented, none of the alleged shortcomings has proven more universally prevalent, and none has been less responsive to alterations within the system than the recurrence of business cycles. Throughout their histories, all capitalist countries without exception have been plagued by the continuous succession of periods of recession, depression, recovery, prosperity, recession, depression—and so on in perpetual, unending economic cycles.

Does all this mean that such business cycles are characteristic of capitalist societies and of capitalist societies alone? Indeed, this is precisely what is meant here. But, to be sure, that certainly could not and does not imply that living standards of average citizens are therefore higher under other economic systems. It is possible indeed for non-capitalist economies (say, for instance, feudal societies) to languish perennially under economic conditions below even the worst that Western market economies experience during their deepest depressions. Could it possibly mean, then, that non-capitalist societies do not have their economic ups and downs? No, it could not mean that either, because all societies, including the leading Marxist-Leninist societies of yesteryear, have had their good times and their bad times, their times of relative plenty, and their times of pronounced shortages. What is meant, then, when it is asserted that business cycles exist only under capitalism?

There is a world of difference between the ups and downs in non-market economies and the business cycles in capitalist economies. Why do people experience periods of especially grave economic deprivation in non-capitalist societies? The answer has always been the same: because there is not enough to go around, not enough to meet their needs. There may have been a crop failure due to a frost, a flood, or a drought; there may have been an earthquake or hurricane that devastated a part of the country; there may have been a war that destroyed homes and factories; there may have been a series of human errors on the part of the planning authorities. But whatever the cause, economic downturns have always occurred when there were great shortages of goods and services available to meet the people's needs. In capitalist societies, on the other hand, the opposite seems to be the case. Periods when goods are in short supply are often periods of prosperity; and depressions usually set in when there are "too many" goods available. In the United States, we experienced our greatest prosperity, up to that time, during the days of World War II. Unemployment was minimal then, young men served in the armed forces while others worked overtime or held two jobs, women entered the labor force in numbers larger than ever before, and few families complained about not earning enough. Those, indeed, were prosperous times. But those were also the times when you had to stand in long lines to get a pound of meat or a package of cigarettes; those were the times when you needed a rationing coupon to be able to buy such ordinary staples as sugar; and new automobiles or nylon stockings were not available at all, for love or money, because steel was used primarily to produce guns and ammunition, and nylon was requisitioned for the manufacture of parachutes. And in the early 1930s when we went through the worst depression in our country's history, when close to one out of every three Americans able and willing to work and eagerly looking for a job could not find employment, and when people were hungry throughout our land: were we unable then, to produce enough to meet our citizens' needs? Certainly not. Already at the end of the First World War, our productive capacity was greater than that of the next four largest industrialized nations—England, France, Germany, and Russia—combined. By the end of the 1920s, we were certainly able to produce enough to provide a comfortable standard of living for all our people. We had the land and the farms to supply us with all the food and raw materials we needed; we had the factories and the machines to turn out the industrial goods we wanted; we had the transportation and communication systems capable of bringing the raw materials to the factories and the finished goods to the consumers; and we had the workers, eagerly willing and able to work and actively looking for jobs; but somehow, the wheels of our economy ground to a halt. The produce on the farms was left unattended, the factories were standing still, and well over a quarter of our labor force was unemployed. So, when a restaurant put a sign in the window that a dishwasher was needed, the lines started forming in the dark of night, and by the time the restaurant opened in the morning, hundreds of people were begging for the job. There was so much wheat that it rotted in the fields of Kansas; but no one bothered to harvest it, while in the cities families lined up at soup kitchens to get a bowl of soup and a piece of bread. There were so many oranges on the trees in California and in Florida that nobody took the trouble to pick them; but in the cities, hungry children were suffering from vitamin deficiencies. There was so much coffee in coffee-producing countries that in Brazil it was actually, literally used as a fuel for locomotives; but in the streets of Chicago and New York grown men were begging for a nickel for a cup of coffee. What had gone wrong?

No indeed, there was no lack of physical and technical ability to produce the goods our people needed; there was nothing wrong with our productive capacity. Whatever had gone wrong was in the area of distribution. Somehow our economic system failed to put into the hands of the American people the purchasing power they needed to buy the goods they had produced at a price that would enable the producers to stay in business. And so, when the price of cotton fell, as indeed it did fall, from a dollar a pound to below a nickel a pound, it didn't pay for the cotton growers in the South to have the cotton picked and ginned and shipped to the North since the price it would fetch wouldn't even pay for the transportation costs from Alabama or Texas to New York.

And in the early 1990s, once again, we had unsalable surpluses, especially in the agricultural sector. Once again, in this the richest country in the world, we had so much food that we didn't know what to do with it; but there was, and still is, widespread hunger and poverty in America. We had so much gas that many producers in Kansas, Nebraska, and Ohio couldn't sell it and had to cap their wells; but during the cold winter months, poor families found their gas turned off for inability to pay their bills unless local "warm hearts" drives collected enough in donations to do it for them. And, almost unbelievably, the creation of artificial shortages to raise or sustain prices is usually offered as a solution to the problem. In the 1930s, while faced with desperate needs of the population, we plowed under every third row of cotton and slaughtered millions of young pigs to restore pre-depression prices. For many years now, the government has paid farmers to keep acreage out of production (although this program is likely to be abrogated in the not-too-distant future). Not so long ago, midwestern dairy farmers poured millions of gallons of milk into the gutter to reduce supplies and maintain prices, and declared their intent to slaughter a good part of their dairy cow herds for the same purpose—all this while, since the beginning of the Reagan-Bush era, hungry children in many places have found their school lunch programs curtailed or suspended altogether.

Why is it that periodically, in capitalist societies, relatively good times are followed by periods of massive unemployment where large numbers of people find themselves in desperate economic straits? The answer is to be found primarily in the economic system itself and in the apparently inevitable maldistribution of wealth and income it engenders. Capitalists (by which we mean, here, the owners of the means of production), obviously, will hire workers and operate their enterprises only if they can make a profit out of their employees' labor. With their earnings, the workers can purchase but a part of the output they produce. Higher income earners, and especially the wealthy few, on the other hand, do not want to spend all their money on consumer goods. Instead, they want to save part of their incomes. As long as these savings are invested in that part of the nation's output that consists of "capital goods" such as new factories, new machines, new tools—as long as they are, so to speak, "recycled"—the economy can continue on an even keel. Workers still have productive jobs, still are able to buy part of the output produced; still try to save a little if they can; and capitalists still consume some of their profits and save and invest the rest. But how long will they continue—how long can they continue expanding productive facilities if they cannot sell all the goods their farms and factories turn out? Inevitably, there comes a time when investments slow down. At this point, some workers are laid off, there is less money available for the purchase of goods already produced, and the economy starts on the downswing—a recurring experience all too familiar to us throughout our history. Then, as more factories cut production or close down altogether, more workers are laid off, more enterprises go into bankruptcy, those still employed—insecure and pessimistic as to the future—postpone purchases; sales drop further, and the recession deepens and turns into a full-fledged depression. Eventually, in time, perishables spoil; other goods are worn out, used up, or discarded; and sooner or later, at the bottom of the depression, some owners of enterprises believe that now things are about to turn around and the market might be ready to absorb some new output. So, they begin hiring workers again, the workers start buying more goods, the capitalists make new investments, and the cyclical upswing gains momentum. But after a while, the economy once again reaches the overproduction/underconsumption phase of the cycle that signifies the beginning of another inevitable downswing.

Economists may argue that this is a somewhat oversimplified presentation and that international exchange rates, the health of the banking system, the economic conditions of our trading partners abroad, and a host of other institutions and occurrences have their impact on cyclical fluctuations. They may argue, correctly, that income-related class structures are no longer as distinct as they were a generation or two ago. Some "workers" (such as well-known actors or sports figures, corporation presidents, and others) may be among the country's top income earners; and some "capitalists" are certainly struggling to make ends meet while many others fail altogether and join the ranks of the workers or the unemployed. Still, the basic principle remains unchanged: recessions and depressions in capitalist market economies are caused largely by what economists have come to call "overproduction" and "underconsumption."

This kind of "business cycle," this kind of recession and depression where people find it impossible to meet their basic needs because there are too many goods (and not too few goods) around, is inconceivable under any economic system other than one based on the profit motive. Could one possibly have imagined a situation in the Soviet Union, in China, or in any of the previously socialist countries where the people would go hungry because there was too much food? It would have been unthinkable for a factory director in the Soviet Union to inform his superior that he is going to shut down his factory and lay off his workers because he can't make a profit. When such a situation occurred, as indeed it often did, the planning authorities would have investigated whether the inability to cover costs was due to inefficiency and, if so, they would have tried to remedy the situation. If this involved the replacement of workers by machines, the workers would have been retrained at the company's (read: the state's) expense, without a day's loss of pay, until they could start their new jobs. If the reason for the failure to operate profitably lay elsewhere (say, for instance, increasing cost of raw materials or fuels), and if the planners did not choose to raise consumer prices or shift capital elsewhere, the enterprise would probably have been given government subsidies or a bank loan. If it was the latter and if, after a number of years, the enterprise couldn't repay the loan, the loan would be canceled. After all, the bank and the enterprise belonged to the same owner—society at large—and losses in one enterprise or even one industry could be offset by planned profits in another. So, bread, milk, children's books, children's shoes, and a host of other goods deemed desirable by the leadership were regularly sold below costs in the Soviet Union, the loss to be made up by higher prices charged on goods deemed less essential or even undesirable, such as vodka. All this certainly reduced efficiency, as we define the term; in other words, it reduced output per worker and per hour of labor time. But whatever else was wrong with the Soviet economy, whatever shortcomings it may have had to cope with (and there were manifestly many), it had always been able to avoid business cycle–type economic fluctuations: there had been no unemployment to speak of from the 1930s to the time of the introduction of reforms in the mid-1980s, although there had certainly been much highly inefficient "underemployment," meaning more workers employed than necessary to perform the required tasks.

Obviously, producers operating in a free-enterprise market economy can never do what Soviet managers did. The American manufacturers of children's shoes cannot stay in business unless they can at least meet costs, and neither can our farmers or the owners of any other productive American enterprises. Nor is it difficult to understand why throughout history and in spite of all efforts, governments in capitalist countries have been unable to remedy the situation—unable, in other words, to eliminate periodic unemployment and inflation or such other corollaries of cyclical fluctuations as widespread business failures or huge deficits.

"Supply-side economics" that would make the rich richer in the hope that some of it would trickle down to the poorer (some like to call it "feeding the horse so that the sparrows may eat") has proven disastrous for the welfare of the great majority, as not only the unskilled and semi-skilled, the sick, the unemployed, and the destitute, but even our farmers and a great number of small business owners discovered in the 1980s. Such "liberal," "progressive" remedies as "New Deals," "Fair Deals," or public welfare–oriented policies in general cannot solve the problem either, but they can at least curtail somewhat the extremes of business cycles by job creation, subsidization of certain enterprises or branches of the economy (such as farming), redistribution of wealth and income (by such means as making taxes more progressive, providing more adequately for the needy and raising minimum wages), and by providing greater economic security—all anathema to conservative defenders of a more self-regulating free enterprise system. Changing interest rates and government spending and taxation policies (tax less and spend more during bad times; do the opposite during periods of prosperity and threatening inflation) can also help mitigate recessions and depressions. Still, as long as the essence of a profit-based economy is retained, all such measures can at best make the patient more comfortable and reduce the pain. American and Western European history has proven over and over that they cannot cure the malady. The recurrence of recessions and depressions—often dubbed "necessary periods of readjustment"—appears to be a price that must periodically be paid for whatever other advantages a capitalist, free enterprise system may have to offer. This being the case, we must at least see to it that these "periods of readjustment" do not bring unbearable hardships to those least able to cope with them.

Chapter 4

Distribution of Wealth and Income: Poverty Amidst Plenty

The extent of poverty in this, still the richest country in the world, is deplorable. The gap between the wealthy and the poor has been widening since the early 1980s; it is larger today than at any time since the Census Bureau began collecting income distribution data in 1947; it is by far the most sizable among all the industrialized countries in the world; and it seems that most of our elected representatives, instead of searching for means to narrow the gap, are wrangling over how much to cut long-existing programs aimed at providing assistance to the needy. On top of that, conservatives are also demanding huge tax cuts which would primarily benefit the wealthy and, if enacted, would further widen the chasm. It hasn't always been that way.

Back in the depression days of the early 1930s, President Franklin Delano Roosevelt talked about one-third of the nation being ill fed, ill clothed, ill housed. But he and most of his followers relentlessly combatted poverty in America. The social policies enacted under Roosevelt's New Deal were expanded under Truman's Fair Deal, Kennedy's New Frontier, and Johnson's vision of a Great Society that encompassed an "unconditional war on poverty." These policies were largely adhered to by the pre-Reagan Republican administrations of the 1960s and 1970s as well. Social security legislation, unemployment compensation laws enacted by each of the 50 states, welfare legislation, antipoverty ordinances, economic opportunity acts, funds for vocational training, establishment of work training camps and centers for underprivileged youth, aid to various community action programs to combat poverty were all aimed at helping low-income and no-income families and individuals to find their way out of indigence.

Even during the Reagan and Bush administrations' relentless on-slaught against all social welfare programs, expressions of deep concern and calls for realignment of priorities could be heard from a wide variety of groups throughout the land. In February 1984, the Citizens Commission on Hunger in New England reported on "widespread hunger in America" and blamed, at least in part, "stingy government policies" for having intensified the hunger problem. America's Catholic bishops, in their annual meeting in 1986, adopted by a vote of 225 to 9 an economic statement decrying the extent of poverty in so rich a nation as "a social and moral scandal that must not be ignored." In October 1987, the Physicians Task Force on Hunger published a report entitled "Hunger Reaches Blue Collar America," and its director, Harvard Professor Larry Brown, asserted that 20 million go hungry at some point each month and that "supply-side economics is a failure as a hunger remedy." The National Academy of Sciences' September 1988 study, entitled "Homelessness, Health, and Human Needs," called the growing number of homeless children "nothing short of a national disgrace." And in late November 1988, in a step never before taken in American history, two former U.S. presidents, one Democrat, one Republican, called on George Bush, the president elect, not only to congratulate him but to present him with an "American Agenda" on which, they hoped, he would base his policies. In their report, Jimmy Carter and Gerald R. Ford told George Bush that they saw "two Americas, one increasingly wealthy, one tragically poor, a land of opportunity for most and of idle hopelessness for too many." And they left no doubt as to the importance they attached to the improvement of social programs, especially those focusing on the health, nutrition, and education of millions of children living in poverty.

Nowadays, the voices raised in defense of the poor and the disadvantaged are fewer, and they are generally more cautious and more subdued. The conventional wisdom, not subscribed to by everyone but by all too many, has it that the poor have mostly themselves to blame for their plight. They are generally portrayed as lazy, drug and alcohol addicted, unsavory characters—true for some, but certainly not for the great majority. They are told to get to work, instead of depending on the public dole, as if there were enough jobs for all of them, as if there were enough affordable daycare centers for their kids while they are at work, and as if the jobs some of them do find paid enough to lift them above the poverty level.

According to a 1998 report by the Census Bureau, the upper fifth of income earners in the United States took home almost one-half of the total income in our country (49.3 percent), whereas the lowest fifth a measly 3.6 percent—a gap between the rich and the poor twice as large as in Germany and three times as large as in Japan. Some 40 million Americans are officially counted as living in poverty, defined for 1999 as having an annual income of under $16,530 for a family of four, correspondingly less for smaller families, and $8,480 for an individual; almost 20 million of the "poorest of the poor" earn less than half that amount. (A September 1998 United Nations Research Report gives the percentage of Americans living in poverty as 16.5 percent, in other words, around 45 million, although their findings show that we lead the world in per capita consumption of goods and services. A U.S. Census Bureau study, also published in September 1998, comes up with a lower figure: 13.3 percent or 36.5 million Americans living below the poverty line. The poverty rate of Afro-Americans, and of Hispanics in any case, is about twice that high.)

People on minimum wage ($4.25 per hour before October 1, 1996, $4.75 after that, and $5.15 since October 1, 1997) still have a gross income of barely $10,700 per year *before* taxes and social security deductions (President Clinton, in his January 1999 State of the Union address, called on Congress to raise minimum wages to $6.15 over a two-year period. Even this increase to a $12,800 pretax annual income would keep the minimum wage earner well under the poverty level for a family of three or four); but the *median* salary including bonuses paid by the 400 largest U.S. corporations to their top executives is over $6,000 *per day*. And some of the highest of these incomes stagger the imagination. Walt Disney's Michael Eisner's remuneration in 1994 was $202 million. Each hour during that year, day and night, awake or asleep, he earned more than an unskilled worker earned in *two and a half years*—and that doesn't even include other income from stock dividends, interest on bonds, and what have you. And while the average salary of top executives of large American corporations is around *140 times* the wage of average workers—a remuneration widely believed to be essential so as to give the CEOs the necessary incentive—German and Japanese CEOs seem to be doing just fine earning 30 times as much as their workers.

What holds true for income inequality holds true even more for accumulated wealth. There were 13 billionaires in the United States in 1982, 13 individuals who owned more than one thousand million dollars; 15 years later, in 1997 there were 170, over 50 of them holding assets of more than five billion. In 1998, the reported net worth of Microsoft's Bill Gates, who tops the list, was an incredible $51 billion. If you earned enough to save $100,000 a year, it would take you half a million years to accumulate that kind of money. The *net worth* of the richest *one percent* of Americans, about 970,000 households in all—the total owned by them minus what they owe in private and business debts—amounted to well over $6 trillion in the mid-1990s, *more than our entire national debt*, more than is owned by the bottom *90 percent*, some 87 million households in our country. And the wealthiest 10 percent own 84% of all stocks, 88% of all bonds, and 91% of all businesses. We are Number One among the industrialized countries in the world in billionaires and in children living in poverty, Number One in wealth and income inequality, Number One in big homes and in homelessness. Not since 1929, the eve of the great depression, has wealth in our country been as unequally distributed as it is in the 1990s. And, according to the Fall 1998 *Statistics of Income Bulletin*, published quarterly by the IRS, almost 1,000 of the highest 1.1 percent of income earners get away with paying no income tax at all!

Most distressing perhaps, and most harmful to our country's future, is the fact that in the past 25 years, the number of children living in families below the poverty line has almost doubled. Today, one out of every five American children lives in poverty, a rate twice as high as in Europe. Among 20 nations in a similar stage of economic development, we rank worst in infant mortality. Our death rate for newborns during their first year of life is 73 percent higher than in Singapore, or Taiwan, and 93 percent higher than in Hong Kong—hard to believe but true nevertheless (just check any reliable source such as the *Encyclopedia Britannica Yearbooks*: Look under "Education and Health" for each individual country); and the outlook is much worse for African Americans. With infant mortality rates double that of whites, a black baby born in an inner city would have a much better chance to survive had it been born in Costa Rica, Cuba, or South Korea. And it goes without saying that it is primarily the babies of the poor who are dying during their first year of life, not merely because of respiratory or heart failure, nor merely because they lack adequate food and shelter but, said former Senator Bill Bradley of New Jersey, "the awful truth is these babies are dying because their mothers cannot afford prenatal care and because the cries of the poor are always the hardest to hear"; and, contrary to public perception, two-thirds of these babies have parents who work at least part time. As a matter of fact, 40 percent of America's poor are working, but don't earn enough—not even on full-time jobs—to make ends meet. It's not just laundry workers, hospital attendants, chamber maids, dishwashers, security guards, and other urban working men and women in low-paying service jobs. The California Institute for Rural Studies finds, for instance, that at least half of that state's farm workers live in poverty. And whatever else you may hear or read, the fact is that it is harder today than it used to be to work oneself out of poverty. The parents and grandparents of the present generation were much more likely to find hard work rewarded by fulfillment of the American dream: home ownership, increasing prosperity, the good life, and the promise of an even better life for their children.

For many of us, these statistics seem hard to believe, yet they are true. You may not come across hunger and deprivation too often, especially if you live in a small city, in a well-to-do suburb, or in some of the wealthier rural areas in the Midwest, but privation and hand-to-mouth existence are all around us. Go to Appalachia, drive on back roads through some of the rural areas of the deep South, stroll along the beaches in southern California, take a walk through the inner city or, for that matter, through the center of Chicago, San Francisco, or Washington, D.C., and you can't miss it. Yes, there is poverty in America. You can find the poor lining up at soup kitchens, rummaging through garbage cans, sitting on sidewalks, cup in hand, asking for handouts. Who are these poor?

Besides the obvious ones—the drug addicts, the alcoholics, the mentally ill—there are the great majority of "others." There are the "working poor" discussed above, with an annual income below the federal poverty level. There are the broken families where the breadwinner died, left, is in jail, or never was there for the children to begin with; families headed by young, unskilled women, or sometimes by the oldest child: more than one-third of them live below the poverty line, raising little ones in roach-infested, dilapidated one-room apartments. There are people with disabilities, all too many inadequately assisted under current public programs. There are the minorities: close to one-third of blacks and Hispanics, and one-half of all households headed by black or Hispanic single women, live in poverty. There are the "new poor," formerly reasonably well paid but currently unemployed white or blue collar workers whose companies have "downsized" their workforce, small farmers who have lost their family farms, and small businessmen and businesswomen who have succumbed to competition on the market place. And from the ranks of those above come the homeless, some but certainly not a majority with serious physical, mental, alcohol, or drug addiction problems.

Homeless in our country number in the hundreds of thousands—a new phenomenon since there were few before 1980. You can find them sleeping in doorways, on sidewalks, on park benches, in subway or railroad stations, wrapped in blankets to keep warm, with all their possessions in a bag or cart next to them; you can see them in the late afternoon or early evening trying to find overnight lodgings that the Salvation Army or some other shelters offer; and once again, it's the children who get hurt the most. A landmark study by Ellen L. Bassuk of Harvard University found that the stress of being without shelter has a devastating effect on children, and she documented widespread sleeping disorders, listlessness, hyperactivity; almost half of homeless preschoolers manifest delays in developmental skills; over 40 percent of homeless school age children have to repeat a grade; one in four is assigned to a class for the handicapped. "Most are potentially normal children," Dr. Bassuk says, "it's tragic for the child, tragic for the parents, tragic for society." But the budget for subsidized housing was cut drastically during the 1980s, and new cuts seem to be in the offing now.

President Franklin Delano Roosevelt once said that "The test of our progress is not whether we add more to the abundance of those who have too much; it is whether we provide enough for those who have too little." Unfortunately, the Reagan-Bush years, and more even, the years of the mid- and late 1990s Republican Congress, have been defined by all-out efforts to dismantle gradually the economic, social, education, and health safety nets so carefully woven during the preceding 50 years.

The detrimental effects of our ever-worsening income inequality have not been felt only by the poor, the unemployed, the welfare recipients. From the end of the 1970s to the mid-1990s real wages (wages adjusted for inflation) and the purchasing power of working families—and especially of low-income working families—have been declining (the minimum wage of $1.60 in 1968 bought as much then as $7.21 did in 1996 when the minimum wage was $4.75 and over four million were working for minimum wages or for less); middle-class incomes have remained virtually stagnant, but corporate profits have soared and the total value of stocks, held predominantly by the wealthy, has increased more than fivefold. (The slight increases in real wages in 1997 and 1998 were the first such increases reported in 20 years so that by the end of the 1990s, the median workers' real wage was still virtually the same as it had been in the late 1970s.) Thus, the great majority of Americans have failed to share in the prosperity and the economic progress reported by our media; and for all too many anxiety, economic uncertainty, discontent, fear, and anger have been taking the place of the optimistic American dreams of yesteryear. Perhaps it is time for America to heed President Kennedy's warning that "If a free society cannot help the many who are poor, it cannot save the few who are rich."

Chapter 5

Inflation versus Unemployment: Which Is Worse?

Economists consider inflation and unemployment the major challenges to a country's economic well-being and stability. But if we have to choose, if to curtail one we have to accept an increase in the other, which is worse for the individuals affected, for society at large?

Since inflation and unemployment affect different groups in society very differently (a tenured university professor, for instance, may not give unemployment a second thought but could be quite concerned about inflation while the opposite may hold true for a factory foreman whose wages have kept up with rising prices but who may worry about his company's downsizing), the reader may reach the conclusion that the answer involves a value judgment, and rightly so. Still, it seems clear, to this author anyhow, that if choose we must, a moderate increase in inflation is immensely preferable to a similar increase in unemployment. Logic, pure and simple, seems to point in that direction. After all, have you ever heard of anyone committing suicide because prices rose by an additional 1 percent? But an increase in unemployment by 1 percent—1,350,000 more workers out of jobs—now that can and does drive many into despair.

Inflation occurs when at prevailing price levels buyers want to purchase more goods and services than are available, thus pushing up prices. (After all, if you own a grocery store and your customers buy all the strawberries you have at 98 cents a pint within a couple of hours, aren't you going to up the price the next day?) Inflation can also be brought on by rising costs of production. (The oil crisis in the 1970s that eventually pushed the price of oil from $3 a barrel to $40, affected costs in virtually all branches of industry.) An increase in the money supply is on rare occasions generated by the Federal Reserve; intended to stimulate a sluggish economy by increasing overall demand, it necessarily puts upward pressures on prices. But whatever the cause, inflation basically refers to rising price levels or, in other words, to a decrease in the purchasing power of money. As the American comedian Milton Berle once put it: "Inflation means that your money will not buy as much as it did during the depression when you didn't have any."

The type of inflation we are talking about here is the type we have been experiencing over the years in this country, "creeping inflation" as economists call it, at rates of 3 or 4 percent or even at rates pacing about at 8, 10 or 12 percent. (In 1998, influenced largely by drastically lower gasoline prices, the overall price level rose by only 1.6 percent, the lowest rate of inflation since the 1960s.) But an unstoppable, galloping, runaway inflation is quite a different matter; that would have a devastating effect on any economy. Let me illustrate it by an actual example, the hyperinflation that hit post–World War I Germany in the early 1920s. To get a picture of the approximate speed at which that inflation progressed, imagine that a loaf of bread costs 85 cents today, $1.50 tomorrow, $17 in a week, $150 in two or three weeks, $16 million three months from now. This might give you a rough idea of the velocity at which that inflation galloped ahead, finally reaching unimaginable heights. At its peak, in 1923, there were in circulation paper-money bills that said: One Trillion Marks. Before the inflation, one trillion marks was the equivalent of $250 billion, equal at that time to the total income of all the people in the United States for a period of five years. At the height of the German inflation, one trillion marks was an amount of money that you gave as a tip to a waiter in a restaurant; it was 25 American cents. Menus in restaurants were likely not to show prices because how much your dinner cost depended on how fast you ate it. At the height of that inflation, major department stores in Germany hired full-time help to do nothing but change prices. Prices were raised, on the average, once every 15 minutes. Businessmen, at the beginning, thought they could do well. With people unwilling to hold onto money that lost value literally every minute, they found that they could sell whatever merchandise they had on hand at what appeared to be fantastic profits. But when they called their wholesalers the following day to reorder they discovered that for the price they had gotten for their merchandise, however monumental it may have been, they could not buy back the raw materials that went into the making of the goods. Eventually, people refused to sell what they had at any price. They might trade for other goods or services, they might accept gold or foreign currencies, but the German mark had for all practical purposes become worthless. Savings were wiped out. Elderly people who had saved all their lives for their retirement years discovered that with their life savings they could not buy one single meal, not even a cup of coffee. The German economy came to a virtual stand-still. Painful government measures were necessary. Eventually, in August 1924, the German Reichsbank issued a new currency, the reichsmark, at an exchange rate of one of the new marks for one trillion of the old.

The United States has never experienced anything approaching hyperinflation, nor do we expect we ever will. Only if we ever reached an economic stage where greatly increased demand could not possibly be met by increased output because we produced at capacity levels would we ever need to be concerned about such a possibility. But nothing like that is likely to occur. Usually, we produce at around 80 to 82 percent of capacity. And the low-level inflations that we have been experiencing throughout most of our history have never posed a significant threat to our economy; "creeping" inflation brought on by rising demand and not by increasing external costs is even deemed beneficial by many if not most economists, since it provides a stimulus to consumers and producers alike. After all, if prices are rising slowly but continuously, aren't you more likely to buy the new house, the new car, or the new machine for your factory now, rather than postpone the purchase until next year? And will that not be a boon to the suppliers of goods and services and to the workers they hire in an economy like ours, all too often plagued by the inability of producers to find buyers for all the goods produced?

After all has been said, there are certain groups in society who find even low-grade inflation detrimental to their economic well-being. Debtors may welcome it since they can pay off their debts with cheaper, easier-to-come-by dollars, but creditors don't appreciate it when they get their loans repaid in dollars of decreased purchasing power; hence, in times of rising prices, they are likely to adjust the interest rates they charge accordingly. Inflation is highly detrimental to people on fixed incomes such as retirees who receive the same dollar amounts each month from their pensions or annuities, no matter how high price levels happen to be. Holders of financial assets—cash, bonds, savings accounts, or insurance policies, for instance—are in a similar boat, and so are individuals or enterprises on the receiving end of long-term contracts. Labor unions signing a three-year wage contract for their workers that doesn't call for annual inflation adjustments also fall into this category. And inflation can also undermine depreciation accounting, when companies amortize machinery and equipment by putting money aside at regular intervals for their eventual replacement, only to discover that when that time comes, costs have risen so much that accumulated funds are insufficient to replace their worn out or outdated capital goods.

In many cases, steps can be taken to avoid or at least assuage the corrosive effects of rising prices. So, to protect the elderly, social security is indexed (meaning payments to recipients are automatically increased at regular intervals to offset price increases) and so are many union contracts. Annuities, instead of paying fixed, unchanged monthly amounts, can be set up to pay out less to begin with but more each year in the future to adjust to anticipated rates of inflation—obviously, though, a hardship at the outset for low-income elderly who find it difficult enough to manage on their unadjusted retirement income as it is; and in a similar vein, companies can and often do exercise foresight in regard to set-aside contributions to sinking funds, so as to make them large enough to eventually pay for anticipated replacement costs. But banks can do little about fixed rate mortgages once they have been set up; borrowers, on the other hand, are somewhat better off since they usually can refinance their mortgages if interest rates decline.

Obviously, inflation bears watching, merits guarded caution, and may even call for the provision of safety nets for some of those adversely affected (to wit, the above-mentioned indexing of social security). But as far as the economy as a whole is concerned, there is no evidence that moderate rates of inflation have ever been the cause of a reduction in the total output of goods and services. Hence, policy makers ought to think twice—if not a hundred times—before running the risk of plunging the economy into a whirlwind of unemployment for the sake of reducing inflationary pressures.

Indeed, unemployment is a quite different matter, for idle workers do mean less being produced and also less purchasing power to buy whatever there is for sale. Official unemployment figures, varying in recent years between 4.5 and 8 percent (4.2 percent in April 1999, a 29-year low), are grossly understating the problem. As defined by the U.S. Department of Labor Statistics, you are counted as unemployed only if you are over 16 years of age, are willing and able to work, are actively looking for a job, and are unable to find one. If you happen to be too sick to work you may be "out of work," but you would not be officially listed as unemployed; neither would be those who, after looking in vain for a job for a long time (say 45-year-old coalminers in areas where coal mines have shut down) have given up—and there are at least 1.2 million of them. If you are merely checking newspaper ads in search of employment you are not deemed "actively looking" for a job and are therefore not officially "unemployed." If you would like to work full-time but have only been able to secure a part-time job, you are among six and a half million Americans who didn't make the unemployment list either, since we do not have a "partially unemployed" category. And because government-released unemployment figures are based primarily on home surveys, they also exclude hundreds of thousands of homeless who are looking for work but are unable to find regular employment. Adding all those would easily more than double whatever unemployment rates the Bureau of Labor Statistics of the U.S. Department of Labor publishes every month. Obviously, these official figures cannot and do not include either the hundreds of thousands who *might* want to work but lack the "being able to" qualifications because they are currently behind bars. And then there are the "underemployed," those who hold jobs that call for qualifications far below theirs and that yield accordingly less in pay. These include many technically fully qualified blue and white collar workers whose services are no longer needed in a highly computerized work environment, and who often have to accept lower-level employment at half their previous pay and less; and they also include a substantial percentage of recent college graduates who find it necessary to take jobs that do not require a college degree.

Not to be ignored is the disconcerting matter of the *distribution* of unemployment. Official unemployment figures are averages and, just as average income figures fail to convey a picture of the plight of the poor and homeless, so do these fail to make us aware of the deplorable effects of joblessness on various groups in our society. Hidden behind these averages are widespread disparities in rates of unemployment among different regions in the country, different occupations, age groups, workers of different racial and ethnic backgrounds, and what have you. When, in recent years, average unemployment rates for the country as a whole hovered around 6.5 and 7 percent they were closer to 4 percent in Kansas and Nebraska, but over 12 percent in the Mississippi Delta, and they reached 30 percent in some California communities. An unemployment rate above 1 or 1.5 percent would be highly unusual for full professors of economics, but 15 percent and more is rather frequent in some industries such as construction; and unemployment among college graduates is generally less than half that of the country's overall average. Unemployment rates among African Americans, counting only those "willing and able to work, actively looking for a job, and unable to find one," are regularly more than twice those of whites; and not long ago, the unemployment rate of African-American teenagers in Dade County, Florida surpassed an almost unbelievable 70 percent.

But there is more. When you read that unemployment stands at, let us say, 6 percent, you might get the impression that with all its shortcomings and limitations, it at least holds true that among those counted as part of the labor force, 94 percent are actively employed all year long. Not so, unfortunately. Joblessness, however counted, affects a much higher percentage of individuals and families. Millions of unemployed workers are hired on a temporary or contingency basis (usually at lower pay and without health care benefits to boot), and find themselves out of work again after two or four weeks on the job; others are laid off for two or three months or discharged altogether and, the labor market being what it is, it may take a while for them to find suitable new employment. During the decade 1986–1996, the average length of unemployment was 15 weeks so that at the official 1996 unemployment rate of 5.6 percent, close to 20 percent of the labor force (28 million workers, not 7.5 million) were without jobs for some time during that year. A seven-part series on layoffs and "downsizing," published in the *New York Times* in March 1996, found that nearly three-quarters of all households had experienced layoffs since 1980, and in one-third of them, a family member had lost a job.

The term "downsizing" found its way into American lingo and new editions of dictionaries at the beginning of the 1990s. It refers to companies permanently reducing their workforce (and not just temporarily laying off employees) to increase efficiency and profits. The numbers are staggering and the effects on those bearing the brunt of it—the employees, many of them ten years, twenty years and longer on their jobs—are truly lamentable. From 1993 to 1996, 15,000 jobs were lost at Lockheed Martin, 17,000 at GTE, 20,000 at Digital Equipment, 50,000 at Sears & Roebuck, 55,000 at AT&T, 63,000 at IBM to name just a few. In 1998 alone, Johnson & Johnson downsized its labor force by 4,100, Exxon and Mobil by 9,000, Boeing by 20,000; and there is more to come. According to current estimates, 90,000 positions per year will be eliminated in 1999 and 2000. Add spouses and children and within five years you have the equivalent of an unemployed metropolis of well over a million inhabitants, a metropolis largely without health insurance and in many cases with retirement funds gone also.

"It's really not all that bad," we are told by corporate executives and conservative congressmen and senators, "if they just try, they can locate other jobs; hundreds of thousands of new employment opportunities start up every year." It's not quite that simple, I am afraid. Many of the "downsized," especially those over 40 or 45, find it difficult to get work. And the younger ones quickly discover that most of these new jobs are low-paying ones in the service sector. A generation ago, displaced workers found it relatively easy to secure employment comparable to the one lost; but these days, factory workers find themselves "Mac-jobbed," as some call it, when they have to trade their $35,000-a-year position for a job flipping hamburgers at five or six dollars an hour; and $40,000- to $50,000-a-year white collar office workers often can do no better than procure jobs as travel agents at half their former salaries, or even as security guards, hospital attendants, or supermarket cashiers at $12,000 or $15,000 a year or less.

It probably holds true that if you have the will, the necessary determination, the stamina, the fortitude, if you follow up on numerous newspaper ads, if you go from fast food establishment to fast food establishment and from filling station to filling station, you will find some kind of a job. But that does not negate the fact that there are some six or seven million more individuals looking for work than there are positions available, so that when you do find employment, someone else will not. And in all likelihood, in the foreseeable future, there will not even be enough new jobs in the service sector each year to make up for the losses in industry, agriculture, and government—a problem augmented by increasing population, and by the growing number of women entering the labor force. Though low by official count in 1998–1999, unemployment and underemployment (lower jobs than one is qualified for, or part-time jobs when one wants to work full-time) may well become the scourge of the twenty-first century.

The detrimental effects of increasing unemployment are well documented. Study after study shows that every increase in unemployment brings in its wake measurable increases in admissions to state prisons and mental institutions, in homicides, suicides, divorces, child abuse, and other family problems. Unemployment also widens the gap between the haves and the have-nots, reduces much-needed medical care for family members, and makes entire families homeless. And as far as the economy as a whole is concerned, any increase in unemployment not only reduces output (the unemployed no longer produce) but results also in additional government expenditures (for unemployment compensation, welfare, food stamps, etc.), in reduced income and sales tax collections (the unemployed don't earn and don't spend the way they used to), and therefore in detrimental effects on government budgets and on our national and state debts.

To put the problem into global context, let us take a quick look at some other countries in similar stages of economic development. Japan enjoyed jobless rates of one-third or less than ours for decades; and when in November 1992 they rose from 2.3 to 2.4 percent, the government introduced a stimulus package of $87 billion (10.7 trillion yen) and another of $117 billion (13.2 trillion yen) four months later—in all more than five times that proposed by President Clinton, approved by the Congress, but filibustered by then minority Republican members of the Senate (although the economic slump of the mid- and late 1990s that eventually spread to most of Asia brought in its wake unemployment rates in Japan, approaching a previously unheard of level of 5 percent). Brought on in part by the domino effects of cautious foreign investors losing confidence and pulling their money out, the age-old capitalist malady of widespread economic deprivation in spite of the presence of means of production more than adequate to meet all people's needs seems to have temporarily won the upper hand. In Europe, on the other hand, the percentage of workers out of jobs is considerably higher than in the United States, around 10 to 12 percent in most countries, but the treatment of the unemployed there is much different from ours. Unemployment is not treated as a failure of the individual but as a shortcoming of society. In France, for instance, unemployment compensation is a respectable percentage of the last wage or salary and depends in part also on length of time worked; it is gradually reduced over five years and if the unemployed still has no job then, as of 1997, welfare sets in at $460 per month for an individual and $690 for a couple, with child care allowances and rent subsidies on top of it. There are government-sponsored training programs for unemployed youths, and to reduce joblessness, the government creates and offers vast numbers of jobs. In this time of high unemployment in the late 1990s, in Paris, for instance, thousands of workers find employment as street sweepers, the garbage is collected daily, and the mail is delivered three times a day. "We did without all that aid in the thirties," commented a former minister and editor of *Le Monde*, "The result was fascism. Never again."

In England, Germany, and Austria the situation is comparable. In Holland and the Scandinavian countries social welfare measures are even more extensive. As just one example, a radio announcer on an Amsterdam radio station, laid off in 1994 after 20 years of service when her station's workforce was downsized, received her full salary for another nine months and unemployment compensation of 80 percent of her salary for six years thereafter.

What are we in our country doing about the problem? What should we do about it?

In recent years, there have been calls for greater corporate responsibility, greater job security for company employees. "Although the national economy has caught fire," said then Secretary of Labor Robert Reich in March 1996, "the gains to many workers have gone up in smoke." And while admonishing workers to seize the opportunity to upgrade their skills, he emphasized that "the business community also has a responsibility to treat workers as assets to develop rather than costs to be cut. Do corporations not have a responsibility to keep workers employed when profits are rising," he asks, "a moral responsibility to upgrade workers' skills, an obligation to fully fund pension plans, to provide health care?"

These are legitimate questions. Many business leaders, however, have a rather different point of view. They argue, and not entirely incorrectly, that corporations are not social enterprises and that it is the primary task of corporate management to earn profits for shareholders. In the short run, they are apparently achieving this goal. Downsizing results in decreasing costs, rising profits, and stock market prices that soar in response to enhanced corporate "efficiency." But this author, for one, cannot conceive of long-run benefits for business or for society as a whole. It isn't merely that insecure workers who have been bearing the entire direct cost of downsizing feel less pride in their work and jobs, less loyalty to their employers, less interest in their company's success; it is also that in the long run, companies, to be successful, must sell their goods; and unemployed workers or even workers fearful that they may lose their job in the near future and not be able to find a comparable new one, are clearly more hesitant buyers.

Could government be a catalyst to help change corporate behavior and attitudes without sacrificing efficiency? Then House Minority Leader Dick Gephardt (D-MO) seemed to think so. Stating in April 1996 that "for too many Americans just staying in place means a never-ending scramble of long hours, second jobs, and credit card debts," he unsuccessfully led the House contingent of a controversial 1996 House-Senate campaign to push through a new corporate code of conduct. The proposed legislation would have provided tax breaks for businesses that avoid mass layoffs and, instead, give upgrade training to their workers.

It seems clear that unemployment is one of the economic problems— and perhaps the major one in our times—that the free market is unable to solve by itself. Once again, government involvement is called for. Although unemployment cannot and need not be pared down to zero, government can still play a paramount role in reducing joblessness. After all, during the days of World War II, unemployment went down to 1.2 percent. Does it really take a war to cope with the problem? This author does not think so. Of course we need not, and probably could not, reduce unemployment to nearly so low a level without extensive government controls and a risk of unacceptably high inflation; nor is that necessary, as long as we do not turn our backs on those who still remain unemployed for a time, however long, without any fault of their own: they and their families (and especially their underage children) must be able to land in a safety net, and not in the gutter. "Doesn't our government recognize the depth of the job crisis in our country? I think not," said Keith Brooks, director of the New York Unemployment Committee in 1994. So what is our government to do?

In a course in introductory economics, you would be taught that we have available what economists call "monetary" and "fiscal" tools to try and curtail unemployment. In our country, *monetary policies* are handled by the Federal Reserve and consist primarily of changing interest rates and bank reserve requirements, and of buying or selling government securities in the open market. If the goal is to reduce unemployment, the Federal Reserve can lower interest rates and reserve requirements so as to make it easier for producers and consumers to borrow money which, once spent, will obviously create jobs; and the FED (Federal Reserve) can buy government securities on the market from the general public, once again placing more spendable money into circulation. The government's *fiscal policies*, based on its power to spend and to tax, would need to follow a similar path. So, if job creation were the goal, proper fiscal policies would call for the government to make more money available by increasing its own expenditures and by reducing taxes so that taxpayers also have more dollars at their disposal to invest or otherwise spend. Obviously, if the perceived goal were to combat inflation, the opposite monetary and fiscal policies would be called for. Hence, the risks of higher rates of inflation must be balanced against the dangerous course of promoting more widespread unemployment. So let us not continue to exaggerate the dangers of inflation while failing to address adequately unemployment whose destructive power over individuals and corrosive effect on the fabric of our society we have all too frequently misjudged and underestimated.

While the monetary and fiscal policies outlined above provide a very general, theoretical framework for action, we should emphasize more specifically and more to the point that our society has countless unmet needs: crumbling roads, bridges, and schools begging to be renovated; millions crying out for adequate housing within their financial reach; single mothers unable to go to work, lest they can find free or low-cost daycare centers for their children; elderly Americans in need of long-term care they can afford without going into destitution. And whether, at the time you are reading this book, our unemployment rate happens to be around 4, 5, 6, 7, or 8 percent, the fact that remains there are millions willing and ready to work for reasonable remuneration. If the private sector, for whatever reason, cannot or will not provide jobs for them, then we should perhaps listen to a proposal made long ago by former senator and vice president Hubert Humphrey that the government be the "employer of last resort" for there is work to be done that would benefit society, and there are the people willing to do it. Some may consider a provision in the 1992 Democratic Party Platform that advocates the establishment of "a national public works, investment and information structure to provide jobs and strengthen our cities, suburbs, rural communities and country" a call for a step in that direction.

Beyond all that, in these technologically advanced times, there is clearly a need for more and not less government-sponsored training and retraining of jobseekers to enhance employability, for youth projects, and for more financial aid for needy, promising, meritorious college students. Programs such as these do not provide an immediate cure-all but are certainly necessary investments in our people (economists call it investments in human capital), bound to pay high dividends in the long run. Will all that not generate new or increase existing annual deficits and further raise our national debt, you might ask. Possibly, though not necessarily so, since increased employment reduces the need for unemployment compensation and welfare payments and raises income and state sales tax collections. But even if it did, is our national debt really as great a danger as it has been made out to be, and should balancing the budget really be our primary economic concern? Let us turn to these issues next.

Chapter 6

Balancing the Budget:
The Cure for Our Economic Ills?

Rhetoric about the paramount importance of balancing the federal budget (keeping annual government expenditures within the limits of revenues collected) has pervaded the American political scene for decades. Franklin Delano Roosevelt campaigned on a balanced budget platform, Eisenhower considered it a necessity, Carter and Reagan promised to achieve it within the first two or three years of their presidency, Bush followed in their footsteps. None of them succeeded, and years that we operated in the black have been few and far apart—less than a handful since the days of the Great Depression in the early 1930s. Sincere men they were all, but they couldn't do it. On the contrary, annual deficits (the amount the federal government spends per year over and above what it takes in) rose substantially during the Carter administration and skyrocketed during the Reagan-Bush years, from $74 billion in 1981 to $405 billion 10 years later, in 1991. A balanced budget has long been easier to promise than to achieve; the last time we had one was in 1969, and none thereafter until the end of the 1990s. President Clinton, upon his reelection in 1996, called it the "top priority" of his second term. Deficits did come down every year during his first six years in office, reaching a low of less than $25 billion dollars in fiscal year 1996–1997—less than 0.5% of our GDP as compared with 4.4% in England, 4.1% in France, 3.8% in Germany, and 6.7% in Italy.

By 1998, huge corporate profits, rising consumption expenditures, and a booming stock market (booming that is, until it started a drastic, if temporary, decline in late August) flooded government coffers with unexpected tax windfalls, resulting in a budget surplus of about $70 billion—the first in 29 years; the president's budget proposal for the 1999–

2000 fiscal year aimed at a surplus of $117 billion; and the non-partisan Congressional Budget Office predicted sizable government budget surpluses for years to come, a prediction supported by most economists and analysts. Still, this author wouldn't bet on it. In any case, for reasons discussed at length below, surpluses will not last forever and sooner or later deficits will reappear. When that time comes, as it inevitably will, would then disaster loom on the horizon? No, I would say. I wouldn't panic about it.

While always deemed important, a balanced budget has during the past 20 or 25 years acquired the validity of an article of religious faith; more than that, it has become an obsession. Its wisdom has been heralded from every political pulpit in the land, and woe to candidates for political office who failed to avow that they would work toward reaching that promised land within the very next few years, and now that it has been reached, to see that it will be maintained. So, toward this end, annual government deficits are to be avoided, and the government is to be mandated (perhaps by an amendment to the Constitution) to spend no more than it collects in revenues during each annual fiscal year period of October 1 of one year to September 30 of the next—no matter what.

Could it be that the dangers of government outlays exceeding receipts have been exaggerated; that, political oratory and "expert" opinions notwithstanding, a rational economic policy may often call for *raising* government expenditures, even if it means sustaining deficits and increasing the national debt? This position, unpopular as it currently may be in the public eye, is actually supported by large numbers of renowned economists, including, recently, the 1996 Nobel Prize winner in economics, William Vickery (who unfortunately died three days after receiving the coveted prize), renowned economists and Robert Heilbroner and Peter Bernstein who, in their 1998 book *The Debt and the Deficit*, advocate, whenever necessary, "a 'deficit' by which we mean growth promoting expenditures on a capital budget of 2 to 3 percent of GNP" ($150–$225 billion in 1998).

There are basically three ways to reduce deficits and embark on the road toward a more balanced budget: decrease government expenditures, raise taxes, or achieve higher rates of economic growth in the private sector that would result in higher tax collections flowing into governmental coffers and in lower rates of unemployment, thus reducing the need for support of the jobless and the poor.

Raising taxes is a definite political no-no; on the contrary, candidates for political office better promise tax cuts unless they want to disregard Franklin Delano Roosevelt's caveat that "the first duty of a politician is to be elected." Higher rates of economic growth alone, which everyone seems to want and hope for, are unlikely to do the job. Annual growth rates of 2.5 or even 3 percent may help to reduce deficits but generally not enough to completely eliminate them; and higher growth rates than that—difficult to achieve as they are—could cause some inflationary pressures, which so concerns the Federal Reserve that it is unlikely to allow them (and seems quite capable of stopping them in their tracks by such monetary policies as raising interest rates). In 1994, when "threatened" by high rates of economic growth, the Fed did exactly that six times in that one year alone (although in 1997, 1998 and 1999, with no inflationary pressures in sight, the FED took the very unusual step of allowing even higher growth rates *for the time being*). So, in essence, to reach and maintain a balanced budget, this still leaves us with reducing government expenditures. But which government expenditures? Our elected representatives in Washington are unlikely to propose cuts in their own salaries. The interest on the national debt is a legal obligation that cannot be touched, reductions in military expenditures are politically risky and therefore likely to be minimal at best (actually, in 1999, President Clinton proposed boosting military spending by $110 billion over a six-year period—a proposal Congress may raise further but will certainly not reject)—and these two alone account for fully one-third of our governmental budget. (After the end of the Cold War, military expenditures were reduced slightly for a decade, but they still amounted to well over a quarter of a trillion dollars in 1998, and they were increased substantially in the 1999 budget.) So, under the glorious banner of a balanced budget, we have been cutting appropriations for the advancement of the nation's education and health, for slum-clearing projects, for the protection of the environment, and even for such relatively low-cost yet important projects as meat inspections and improving air and job safety. But over half of our government's annual outlays go for social security, medicare, medicaid, and welfare, and therefore major cuts must necessarily come from these "entitlements," in other words, primarily from aid and assistance to the needy, the elderly, the sick, and the disabled. (The most fervent advocates of substantial cuts like to emphasize that what they propose are not actually cuts in the programs but *merely* reductions in their growth rates. Technically they may be correct; but as population increases and as prices go up every year, appropriations must necessarily be raised accordingly to keep at least the same level of services provided. Hence a cut in *planned* growth rates of such programs, in fact, amounts to an *actual* cut in per capita services offered.)

Now that a balanced budget has been achieved, will we be able to maintain it over the long haul? Unfortunately, the answer is most definitely "no." Although difficult and probably painful, we know that it is possible to keep government expenditures at or below revenues collected for one or even for a few years. So why not in the long run?

Virtually every year, titanic floods, roaring forest fires, devastating earthquakes, and hurricanes and tornadoes exact a fearful toll from some parts of our country. When such natural disasters occur, no one denies the urgent need for help, nor the duty of the federal government to provide it. But if the budget is to stay balanced, if the government is not allowed to borrow, and if it is encumbered by the constraints of political, social, and economic reality from raising taxes, how will we pay for it? Must we, can we again cut entitlements and make those least able to afford it carry the burden and foot the bill? Or could a case be made that balancing the budget need not necessarily be our top priority?

Yes, random acts of nature may cry out for immediate government action. But there is more. The humming economy—the longest uninterrupted period of economic prosperity since the end of World War II— will not last forever. We all are well aware that our country periodically goes through periods of recession and depression. When they occur, as they have throughout our history, when unemployment increases, businesses fail in large numbers, and the economy is on a downswing, when the need for government aid and assistance rises dramatically and income tax collections slow down, how will we balance the budget then? Cutting expenditures or raising taxes at such times—in other words, reducing money available to the general public—will only deepen the recession and make matters worse. Even balanced budget advocates begin to understand this when the occasion arises. Roosevelt may have promised in his 1936 campaign that "the budget will be balanced for the fiscal year 1937–1938"; but when recession reoccurred and unemployment rose to 19 percent in 1938 he had second thoughts. "A balanced budget isn't putting people to work," he said, "I will balance the budget as soon as I can take care of unemployment." With a war on his hands a year later, he never did. Eisenhower, when faced with a recession in 1953, expressed identical views. "Balancing the budget will always remain a goal of any administration," he said, "but that does not mean all things must give before a balanced budget. When it becomes clear that the government has to step in, as far as I am concerned, the full power of the government, of government credit, and of everything the government has will move in to see that there is no widespread unemployment." And presidents after him, from Kennedy to Carter and from Reagan to Bush, felt obliged to renege on plans and promises and to submit unbalanced budgets to Congress year after year. No indeed, balancing the budget no matter what, and keeping it balanced over the long haul is not merely unwise economic policy; it will also, I predict, prove unachievable.

Why, anyhow, do people expect the government to balance its budget when they don't balance theirs? They don't when they buy a new car and pay for it over two or three years, when they take out a 30-year mortgage on their home, when, as students, they get loans to go to college. Why do we think it's so wonderful when *corporations* borrow money to build a new factory or open a new retail outlet in our community but so terrible when the *government* borrows to invest in the protection of the environment, the education of our children, or the health of our infirm? Throughout our history, our government has borrowed money to invest in the future of our people. The Louisiana Purchase created a large debt for our young nation but it doubled the size of our country. Should we not have bought the land from France? When our collective security and the collective security of the rest of the world was threatened in World War II, we borrowed at unparalleled levels to pay for the war effort. The result was not only the defeat of the Nazi and fascist war machinery, but also our emergence from the Great Depression and an unprecedented wave of prosperity. Were we wrong to have borrowed money for this national emergency? Since the end of World War II, we have engaged in virtually continuous deficit spending. The result was not economic decay but the longest depression-free period in our history. None of the nine recessions since the end of World War II were the result of excessive government spending; on the contrary, all of them followed years when government deficits constituted a smaller (not larger) part of our national income than previously. It remains to be seen how long the prosperity of the 1990s will survive in the post-1998 budget-surplus era.

We simply cannot go on the way we have in the past, balanced budget advocates tell us; deficits year after year, that's a road to disaster. When the government keeps borrowing huge amounts, they contend, this increase in the demand for money will result in higher rates of interest, by absorbing available funds it will crowd out investments in the private sector, and all these government expenditures will necessarily bring on drastic increases in consumer prices. They sound the alarm; they forebode a dismal future lest we heed their warning. But the fact is that this sequence of events has never happened in American history. During the eight years of the Reagan presidency we increased our national debt from $1 trillion to more than $2 trillion; in other words, by more than the total debt that had been accumulated during the preceding 200 years of our history, and we almost doubled it again during the following four years of the Bush administration. But interest rates and rates of inflation dropped dramatically! And historically, larger deficits that place more purchasing power into the hands of the American people have always spurred on, rather than crowded out, profit-seeking private investments.

In recent years, the most ardent champions of a balanced budget in Congress have pursued an incredible but politically understandable path. Although our military expenditures are almost as high as those of all the rest of the world together, they proposed giving our armed forces several billions more than the generals asked for; although the gap between the rich and the poor in our country is already greater than in any other industrialized country, they proposed tax cuts that would mostly benefit the wealthy; and so, to balance the budget, they have asked sacrifices almost exclusively of the most vulnerable, the politically most defenseless, the ones who do not have PACs (political action committees) or lobbyists to plead their cause. Targeted for drastic reductions or total elimination were 170 programs including summer job programs for inner city youths, Headstart designed to help poor preschoolers on their way, energy assistance to low-income families to keep their homes warm on cold winter days, legal aid that makes legal advice and lawyers available cost-free to low-income families involved in civil suits (such as disputes with their landlord), school lunch programs that often provide the only decent meal for the children of the needy, student loans once called an "investment in our future," social services for *legal* immigrants—the future citizens of our country, the earned income credit that gives tax relief to the most needy of our *working* people, and what have you. And the "moderates" seem to follow in their footsteps, merely softening the blows and assuaging the pain by reducing the most Draconian cuts to still harsh but more manageable magnitudes.

When the budget balancers aver that what they are doing is really for the good of our children, that's the equivalent of asking us to tell our children that, for their benefit, we are not going to borrow money by increasing the mortgage on our house, and that to reduce expenses we will cancel their health insurance, stop giving them money to go to college, and cut drastically their expenditures in order to keep parks and playgrounds in good condition and our air and water as clean and pure as possible in the modern age. You see, the fact is that without past deficits, our children could not have the schools, the highways, the airports, the parks now in existence. If their parents would have had to dig into their pockets to pay for all this by higher taxes, on a pay-as-you-go basis, they would not have been able to buy the houses, the food, the medical care they enjoy. No indeed, if we want to build a good future for our children we must follow a different path. We must give them top education, provide all necessary health care, a safe environment, and funds for research for the development of advanced technology. This, not blindly balancing the budget, will cement our children's future.

Not satisfied with promises and efforts to reach a balanced budget (before we actually did in 1998) and doubtful whether present and future presidents, senators, and representatives will stick by their guns when push comes to shove, budget balancers in Congress have long wanted to make it *legally mandatory* for the federal government to keep annual expenditures within the limits of actual receipts. Toward this end, they have been proposing a balanced budget amendment to the Constitution. In 1995, and again in February 1997, they failed by a single vote in the Senate to reach the required two-thirds majority. Although their voices are temporarily muted by present budget surpluses, we haven't heard the end of it, you can bet on that. (If ever adopted by a two-thirds majority in the House and the Senate, it would subsequently take ratification by three-fourths of the states for the amendment to become part of the Constitution.)

About 11,000 amendments have been proposed since the Constitution was framed in 1789; so far, only 27 have been adopted (and that includes the first ten, the "Bill of Rights," ratified in 1791); but if this one ever became law it would surely bring on the most radical change in the structure of our government since its inception. Widely backed in Congress, and apparently also by public opinion, its advocates, I fear, are not fully cognizant of its ramifications and what its consequences would be.

Let's assume for a moment that the amendment were in place, that after months of haggling and debating Congress finally approved a balanced budget, the president signed it—and then tax receipts fell short of expectations. Presumably, the constitutional amendment would require that Congress now start the whole tormenting process all over again. To cope with the problem of receipts insufficient to meet planned expenditures, some congressmen and senators would propose an increase in income taxes for the wealthiest 5 percent of Americans; some would like to raise gasoline taxes instead; others, opposed to any tax increases, would urge cuts in allocations for health, education, and welfare; yet others would press for reductions in our financial commitments to countries abroad. They wouldn't be likely to reach an agreement, surely not quickly, and if they didn't, then what? Since this is no longer merely a legislative but a constitutional issue, the case would most likely be turned over to the courts. By the time the Supreme Court straightened things out three or four years down the line. . . . well, you get the picture. In January 1997, 1,060 economists, among them 11 winners of the Nobel Prize, signed a letter to Congress calling the amendment "unsound and unnecessary."

But is there no "safety net" built into this proposed amendment, no way out in such a case, or, even worse, in the case of an unexpected national emergency or a deepening recession that seems to get out of hand, you may ask. There is, but you judge whether it is satisfactory. The proposed amendment includes a provision that when a financial exigency seems to call for unfunded government expenditures, the government can borrow money, as long as such a step is approved by 60 percent of both houses of Congress. If you have ever noticed how difficult it is to break a filibuster in the Senate (that takes 60 percent) or a presidential veto (that takes two-thirds of both houses), you'll understand the problem. A minority of 41 percent in *either the House or the Senate* would be able to stop needed expenditures, thereby denying the government the power to provide necessary protection and meet crises head-on, as they occur. Even if the president and the majority could, after prolonged discussion, convince 60 percent of the members of each house that action is called for, it may well be too late to deal effectively with many a troublesome situation at hand. To tie the hands of our elected representatives in such a manner is unconscionable and counterproductive.

Since I have tried to make a strong case against a policy of balancing the budget without regard to circumstances, you may have gotten the impression that I, and other economists who share my views, advocate wild, unrestrained government spending without any consideration to what some term "fiscal responsibility." This surely would be a misinterpretation of our position. We certainly like to see deficits reduced or eliminated altogether when economic conditions call for it, such as during prosperous times, accompanied by relatively full employment. Even at other times, we do not counsel ignoring deficits, and we are acutely aware that they need to be kept within reasonable limits, so as not to allow the growth of our national debt to exceed the growth in our national output and income. But after all has been said, we do believe that the dangers ensuing from deficit spending have been grossly exaggerated, and that they must be carefully weighed against our country's social and economic needs. It makes little sense, I would think, to sacrifice pressing exigencies, necessary investments in our country's future, and the maintenance and protection of our infrastructure on the altar of a balanced budget. Perhaps an allegorical tale could further illustrate and elucidate this knotty problem:

To Balance or Not to Balance the Family Budget

The Millers have three teenage children, John, Susan, and Fred. Fred has a term paper to type, but he is a poor typist. So he asks his sister, Susan, to type it for him. "Gladly," she says, "but that'll cost you five dollars." Fred doesn't have five dollars, so he goes to his dad and explains the situation. His dad willingly lends him the money, and he pays Susan for the typing job. Susan's bicycle is out of commission and she doesn't know how to fix it, but her brother John, who is studying to become an engineer, is good at that kind of thing. She asks him to help her out, but he wants five dollars to do it. Since she now has five dollars, she pays him and he fixes her bike. It's John's turn to mow the lawn, but he has a heavy date that evening and doesn't want to get all tired and sweaty. So he asks his brother Fred to do it for him. Fred does it—for five dollars, of course, and then repays the loan to his dad.

A similar situation occurs in the Smith household. Here, Rita has a term paper to type and her brother Richard is the good typist. But when she goes to ask her father for a five-dollar loan, he looks at her in dismay. "Now wait a minute, young lady," he says. "I don't believe in borrowing money and going into debt. I believe in balancing the budget, for our government as well as for our family.

No loans from me, that's for sure. If you don't have it, don't spend it. Work for it first, earn it, and THEN spend your own money, not someone else's."

Which family is better off? In the first family, the paper was typed, the bicycle fixed, the lawn mowed; in the second family, the budget stayed balanced but nothing was done. You be the judge!

Now wait just a cotton-picking minute, you might say. In this example the loan is paid off, but that's not what our government does. Our national debt already exceeds $5.5 trillion, it has increased fivefold in less than 20 years, and if it keeps rising the way it has . . . ? No country can live with a debt like that. That must drive us into bankruptcy.

Is that really so? Does our national debt really threaten our economic survival, or is this also an exaggerated call to arms, another "conventional wisdom," believed by one and all, but not necessarily quite so? Let us take a closer look.

Chapter 7

Our National Debt: Are We Going Broke?

Our national debt currently stands at over $5.5 trillion. MORE THAN FIVE AND A HALF TRILLION DOLLARS! That's a lot of money.

Every day we read in newspapers and magazines, we hear on the radio, and we see on television, reports involving billions and trillions of dollars. A Seawolf submarine costing $1.5 billion, Perot being worth $3.3 billion, our country's imports exceeding exports by $10 or $12 billion or more in a single month, Microsoft's Bill Gates' wealth surpassing $51 billion in 1998, our government's annual deficits up to $402 billion not long ago, annual government expenditures of over $1.5 trillion, and our country's income and output over $7.5 trillion per year. We have learned to ingest such numbers, but can we possibly have even the slightest inkling of how much money that is?

Billions and Trillions*

Actually, even one billion dollars, ONE THOUSAND MILLION DOLLARS, is an amount of money so large that it simply staggers the imagination. Let me illustrate. Suppose you had been born on the day Christ was born, that you were still alive today, and that you had been able to save money at the fantastic rate of one cent for every second that you lived, that is, sixty cents for every minute, thirty-six dollars for every hour, or 864 dollars for every day of your life during these past two thousand years. At that rate, it would take you another thousand years to save one single billion dollars. One billion seconds ago, John F. Kennedy had just been assassinated, Lyndon B. Johnson had assumed the Presidency, and

---

*An earlier version of "BILLIONS AND TRILLIONS" was published under the title "$1,000,000,000,000. Do You Have Any Idea How Much Money That Is?" in the May 1986 issue of the now defunct *Republic* [Airlines] *Magazine.*

Richard Milhous Nixon—having lost his race for governor of California—had announced (prematurely) his political retirement: One billion minutes ago, Nero had just burned down Rome and Jesus Christ had died on the cross less than a hundred years before; one billion hours ago, people lived in caves and the first written language was still more than one hundred thousand years away; but one billion dollars ago, in terms of government expenditures, was last night.

If one billion dollars is such an incomprehensibly large sum, how can the human mind possibly conceive of the purchasing power of one trillion dollars— ONE THOUSAND BILLION DOLLARS or ONE MILLION MILLION DOLLARS? Such an amount of money is virtually beyond our comprehension. Can you imagine that if you had a stack of thousand-dollar bills four inches high, you would be a millionaire, but a trillion dollars would be a stack of thousand-dollar bills that would reach sixty-three miles into the sky. Or, for perhaps an even more dramatic illustration: A million dollar bills, laid end to end, would just about cover the distance from New York to Philadelphia; a billion would span the earth four times around the equator; but a trillion dollars would stretch more than two hundred times to the moon and back.

To get a picture of how much a trillion dollars can buy, let me make up an example using the Midwest, where I live, as an illustration: With that amount of money, one trillion dollars, we could build a modest seventy-five-thousand-dollar house, place it on five thousand dollars worth of land, furnish it with ten thousand dollars worth of furniture, put a ten- thousand-dollar car into the garage—and we could give all this to each and every family throughout a six-state midwestern region—to each and every family, to be more precise, in Kansas, Missouri, Nebraska, Oklahoma, Colorado, and Iowa. After having done all this, we would still have enough money left out of our trillion dollars to build a ten-million-dollar hospital and a ten-million-dollar library for each of two hundred and fifty cities and towns throughout the six-state region. After having done all that we would still have enough money left to build five hundred schools at ten million dollars each for five hundred communities in this region. And after having done all that, we would still have enough left out of our trillion to put aside at six percent interest (approximately the percentage you could get on long-term government securities in 1998) a sum of money that would pay for all times to come a salary of thirty thousand dollars per year for an army of ten thousand nurses, the same salary for an army of ten thousand teachers, and an annual tax-free cash allowance of three thousand dollars for each and every family throughout that six-state region—not just for one year, but forever.

Annual interest on our national debt is over $250 billion, the debt itself in the trillions: no wonder we are concerned, and understandably so. Yet, before panicking, we need to put it all into perspective. Enormous as our national debt is in actual dollars, does it really represent an unbearable and intolerable burden on us? Is it actually a threat to our and our children's economic well-being and security? Let's take a closer look.

To begin with, the $5.5 trillion owed is a *gross* debt; in other words, it is the total owed by the government (and therefore, collectively, by us, the American people) without deducting anything owned. If you owed $1 million on a mortgage and the property was worth $3 million, would you consider yourself on the edge of bankruptcy? Well, the fact is that the U.S. government holds title to vast properties: over 400 million acres of land—close to one-fifth of the entire land mass of the United States, 400,000 housing units, four times the office space in our ten largest cities, 437,000 vehicles, not counting the military. The U.S. Navy alone must be worth a trillion or two, if not more. Not that I suggest that the government sell the U.S. Navy to pay off the debt. But should we not give some consideration to what we own when we talk about the enormity of what we owe?

More important than accumulated wealth, when weighing the burden of a debt, is income. Suppose you know a man who is in debt to the tune of $250,000—let's say $250,000 net debt over and above what he owns, not gross debt like ours. Is he in financial trouble? You can't answer the question without knowing what his annual income is, can you? If he earns $35,000 per year, you wouldn't want to be in his shoes; but, if his annual income is, let us say $2 million, now that's a different story altogether, isn't it? Our nation's income is best measured by our GDP, our gross domestic product, the total value of all goods and services produced in our country over a period of a year. As of 1998, our national debt was approximately 70 percent of our GDP. While this percentage is twice as high as it was a quarter of a century ago, few people realize that at the end of World War II, in 1946, a period of great prosperity, it was 127 percent of that year's GDP (equal, in other words, to our country's total output over a period of one and a quarter years). Our national debt's effect on the economy is comparable to that of a family with an annual income of almost $80,000 and a mortgage debt of $55,000—usually quite an affordable scenario. And the interest on the debt we have to come up with every year amounts to less than 3 percent of our GDP—high enough, but surely a much smaller percentage of income than the average American family pays annually on its mortgage interest alone.

In some sense even more important, does the burden of a debt not depend also upon to whom you owe the money? If you owe money to your bank and you can't meet the payments, you are in trouble. But it isn't quite the same, as far as family well-being is concerned, if you owe that money to your wife, your husband, or your parents, is it? After all, if you make a payment to your spouse, your family's purchasing power remains unchanged, whether the money stays in your bank account or is transferred to hers. Well, most of our national debt is owed by Americans to Americans: it is owed collectively by the people of the United States to the holders of government securities (such as government bonds, treasury notes and treasury certificates), and 83 percent of these government securities are held by Americans. As a matter of fact, as of

1996, over $1.3 trillion of these government securities—close to a fourth of the total—were held by federal agencies and trust funds, nearly half a trillion of it by the Social Security Trust Fund alone. Add to this well over $400 billion held by state and local treasuries and close to another $400 billion by the Federal Reserve banks and you have over 40 percent of all our domestically held debt accounted for; the rest is in the hands of American citizens, of banks, of insurance companies, of other business enterprises and of such non-profit institutions as universities, charities, and pension funds in the United States. So, more than four out of every five dollars we owe is held within our country, and more than four out of every five dollars we, as taxpayers, pay in interest, flow into American pockets and increase the purchasing power of American citizens, institutions, enterprises, and of federal, state and local government agencies.

"But we are passing this enormous debt on to our children; they and their children, our grandchildren, will have to pay for it," so the media and our government officials often warn us. Once again, this is only a half-truth, at best. For every debtor there is a creditor. So yes, we do leave our children a debt; but we also leave them the corresponding assets, the treasury certificates, the treasury notes, the government bonds which are as good and as valuable as any bank account, any insurance policy, as good as any cash they inherit. And while part of the government expenditures financed by the debt went for consumption (such as food stamps for the needy or transportation costs for the president and his staff from Washington to the Camp David retreat), part of it was invested, for instance, in our educational system, in the protection of the environment, in government-financed medical research—and our children will inherit all this also. Yes, as taxpayers they'll have to pay the interest on our national debt, but as holders of government securities they, their banks, and their institutions will receive all but the 17 percent of it that is held by foreigners.

To fail to meet our country's current needs, to deprive our present generation and especially our poor, including their children, of basic needs for the sake of presumed benefits for future generations is a dubious proposition, to put it mildly. If we could wave a magic wand and wipe out our national debt, the non-bond-holding taxpayers would be slightly better off, but the American holders of government securities would be correspondingly poorer, for these securities represent real, interest bearing assets to them.

So, in essence, the threat posed by our national debt to our economic security and well-being has been grossly exaggerated, not just in recent years but for over half a century. When the debt increased more than fivefold during the days of World War II, from $48 billion to $269 billion, we were told that no country can live with such a huge debt. When our debt approached $1 trillion in 1980, Ronald Reagan, in his campaign for the presidency, sounded the alarm, forecasting economic disaster if we allowed the debt to grow any further—and then it more than doubled during the eight years of his administration, without any of the adverse effects predicted.

Alexander Hamilton said in 1781 that "a national debt, if not excessive, will be for us a national blessing." And so it frequently had been, when deficits that increased that debt helped us cope with recessions and their aftermaths, saw us through wars such as the Civil War and World Wars I and II that threatened our survival as a nation, and enabled us to assist regions in our country at times of natural disasters. Thus our nation's debt has been increasing every year, and it will continue to increase for years to come, even if we continue to balance the budget for the time being. If you are puzzled, let me explain that this is so because the government uses surpluses accumulating in government trust funds, such as the Social Security Fund, for other expenditures. Money so taken is then replaced by government IOUs, and the transaction is treated as simply shifting funds within the government, without referring to such action as deficit financing (an issue taken up in greater detail in Chapter 8 on social security). But the question is: Is our national debt now becoming "excessive"?

"No," I would have to say. True, in number of dollars our national debt is huge, but so is our country's wealth and income and our ability to pay for it. Its current level is not excessive; it's a smaller part of our total income than that of many of the other major industrialized countries in the world; currently, it does not represent a real economic problem, and there is not evidence that it ever has harmed our economy in any way. The annual interest on it is certainly manageable (3.1 percent of GDP in 1998 and projected to go down to 2.1 percent by 2003 as our output and income grow); and, as discussed above, it actually provides an important source of income to millions of individuals and many sectors in our economy. Yet after all has been said it's still true that we do not want to see the debt get out of hand, that we do not want it to grow faster than our national output and income, lest it *could* become an excessive burden in the future. But, as a matter of fact, as our nation's income and wealth increase, which they do virtually every year, we could still afford *reasonable* increases in our national debt, when called for by economic circumstances. What we *cannot* afford is to neglect our country's serious economic problems in such areas as unemployment, health care, education, preservation of the environment, and the like. So it's not that the debt doesn't bear watching at all; it's that it certainly is not the dangerous monster it's made out to be. Let's put it into proper perspective.

Chapter 8

Social Security: Will It Be Here for Our Children?

A free market in and of itself does not and cannot vouchsafe economic security for the elderly who are past their working years. Before the mid-1930s, retirees who had not been able to set aside enough for their old age had to look to their children for support or were left to shift for themselves. No wonder that they constituted a major part of the poor in our country. Then, impelled by the Great Depression of the 1930s, the Social Security Act was passed in 1935 and it provided barebones benefits to retired workers (in 1940, the 220,000 covered retirees averaged benefits of $157 per year). During the first 15 years of its existence, the Act came under bitter attack. Alf Landon, the 1936 Republican presidential candidate, called the Social Security Act "a cruel hoax . . . unjust, unworkable . . . and wastefully financed." And some members of the 1935 Congress predicted that "the act would bankrupt either the government or the moral fiber of our citizenry." But social security became the crown jewel of Franklin Delano Roosevelt's New Deal. Over the years, dollar benefits were increased, coverage was extended to dependents survivors, and disabled people, and social security checks were protected from inflation by annual benefit adjustments. Over 60 highly successful years, it has greatly reduced poverty among the elderly and formed the foundation on which the majority of Americans build protection for the retirement years. In 1998, social security (the "Old Age, Survivors, Disability and Health Insurance Program") sent out $380 billion in checks to 44 million Americans, three-fourths of them retirees and their dependents, the rest survivors and the disabled; and the elderly are no longer the poorest in our society—the children are.

The Social Security Fund has at present (1999) a surplus of over $650 billion and currently collects about $85 billion more each year than it pays out. Both major political parties praise social security and assure us that their only interest is in preserving it for future generations; yet, they tell us drastic reforms are called for because social security is in a stage of "crisis." Let us investigate whether that is really so and, if there is something to worry about, what steps should sensibly be taken to deal with the problem.

Social security is not a government handout. It is a kind of insurance program that provides monthly retirement benefits commensurate with contributions, although, to assure minimum security for all, it pays out a higher percentage of previous income to low- than to high-income earners. It is financed by a payroll tax, as of 1999 6.2% of incomes up to $72,600 paid by the employee and matched dollar for dollar by the employer (an additional 1.45% likewise matched by the employer, is collected for medicare benefits, an issue to be taken up later, in Chapter 10 on health). In a sense, social security acts as an intermediary to assure that current workers pay for their elderly parents (or grandparents) in the expectation that their children and grandchildren will do the same for them. But although workers still contribute considerably more every year than is disbursed, there is a problem—not a crisis, don't panic, but a problem, nevertheless, that has to be addressed.

The situation is different today than it was when social security was first started over 60 years ago. In the 1930s, many more contributing workers didn't even live to retirement age, those male workers who did retired at around 69 years of age and had a life expectancy of 8 more years. Nowadays, the average retirement age is 64, male retirees have 19 more years to look forward to, female retirees 23 or 24. In 1937, there were about 11 contributing workers for every retiree receiving benefits; in 1969 there were 4; today there are still over 3; but with the first of the 76 million baby boomers reaching retirement age in 2011, there'll be only 2 by 2030. (From 2011 on, every seven and a half seconds, another baby boomer will blow out 65 candles; and 1 in 4 of them is expected to live to age 85 and beyond.)

Under the circumstances, and without any changes, the Social Security Fund will obviously not be able to continue accumulating surpluses forever. It is anticipated that by 2015, payouts will begin to exceed social security taxes collected, thus reducing the holdings of the Fund, which by then will have grown to almost $3 trillion. Current projections hold that if things are left as they are, the Social Security Fund will run out of money by 2034.

In the 1930s, the money collected in social security contributions went right out to recipients. By the mid-1960s, social security started accumulating $2 billion in annual surpluses. Then, in 1967, when the Vietnam War caused a $15.7 billion deficit, the largest since World War II, a new government bookkeeping system was introduced. Ever since, under this new "unified budget" method, the government has appropriated social security surpluses for general current expenditures, and it has replaced the money so borrowed from the Social Security Fund with government IOUs thereby masking real government deficits. No wonder the dooms-day prophets talk about a social security "crisis." Comes the second dec-ade of the twenty-first century when social security outlays are predicted to exceed intakes, they warn us, the government will have to start re-deeming its IOUs, and there simply will not be enough money to do so. So convincingly have they presented their arguments that, one survey has it, more young Americans today believe in UFOs than in the survival of social security. But are these doomsday prophets right? Is there a disastrous storm brewing on the horizon, a handwriting on the wall? Is the end of social security in sight?

No, they are not right; such fears are totally unwarranted. There is no reason to panic. If you hold a government bond that is to mature in 15 or 20 years, do you think for a moment that the government may not pay it off? Of course not. Our government securities are the safest in the world. Banks, insurance companies, corporations, state and local agen-cies, charitable organizations, and millions of American citizens are not afraid that they will lose the trillions of dollars they have invested in them. And why should they be? Our government has never defaulted on any of its obligations throughout our history. Why should we assume that it will start doing so in the twenty-first century? Certainly, the money will have to come from somewhere, from higher revenues when more people are at work during prosperous times, from higher tax rates, from cuts in other government expenditures, from the government bor-rowing from elsewhere. But that has always been true. Whenever gov-ernment debt matures, and that happens to the tune of billions each and every day of the year, the government has to redeem its securities; so the government simply issues and sells new government bonds or treas-ury notes and certificates to pay off the ones that have come due. And if the government ever were to default on its obligations—something that is truly inconceivable—the Social Security Fund would be the first to be bailed out; tens of millions of elderly voters would see to that, and their children would be likely to support their parents on this issue.

No, social security is not in a crisis. Until 2034, there is enough money to meet all payments in full. Even if nothing were done at all, enough would still be taken in in social security taxes to meet 77 percent of all benefits for at least the 40 years following, and after that 70 percent for a number of additional years. *But that's only if nothing were done.* A few minor adjustments in the present system could solve all problems for a long, long time.

We could, for instance, increase contributions by employees and employers. (They have gone up. Social security taxes withheld from employees' paychecks and matched by their employers were 1 percent in 1940, and they have continued to climb over the years. Jimmy Carter raised them sharply, and they kept going up from 4.95 percent then to the current 6.2 percent, in effect since 1990.) Present estimates have it that if we increased them by 1.1 percent, from 6.2 percent to 7.3 percent, this small step alone would keep the Social Security Fund solvent for 75 years. Outrageously high social security contributions? Not at all. They are considerably higher in most industrialized countries in the world. While we collect a total of 15.3 percent of income in social security and medicare taxes (half from the employee and half from the employer), Sweden takes in over 30 percent, Germany, the Netherlands, and Spain over 36 percent, and Belgium a grand total of 47.3 percent, three-fourths of it from the employer. Or we could raise the maximum amount of wages and salaries on which social security is collected—a level increased every year anyhow, according to the rate of inflation; (from $3,000 in 1940 to $72,600 in 1999); but we could raise it much more drastically, perhaps from the present level to $100,000 or more. We could raise the retirement age, currently at 65, and we have started doing this also. With health and life expectancy greatly increased, we began to adjust it in 1983: those born between 1943 and 1954 will have to wait until they are 66; this is gradually increased so that those born after 1960 will not qualify for full benefits until they are 67. We could easily extend this to 70 years of age (although some would argue that forcing nurses, waitresses, bricklayers, firefighters, and others to work until 70 is rather drastic, might in some cases be outright dangerous, and that if incomes rise in the next century and we take appropriate steps, we should be able to afford lower, not higher retirement ages). To expand the basis of social security tax collections, we could bring 3.7 million state and local government employees not currently covered into the system; and we could levy social security taxes not only on wages and salaries, but also on such other incomes as rent, interest, royalties, and the like. For the past few years close to one-fourth of social security recipients—the ones with the highest total incomes—have had to pay income taxes on between 50 and 85 percent of their social security benefits. These taxes, which are currently going into the government's general tax receipts could, and probably should be put into the Social Security Fund. What we are doing now is simply transferring money from the Social Security Fund, via the retired taxpayer, into the general tax fund. Actually, it would even make sense to tax social security benefits the same way we tax other pensions at regular income tax rates, as long as the money so collected is put back into the Social Security Fund. A general means test, on the other hand, that would deny all or most benefits to the wealthiest would probably be considered unfair by those affected, and it would run into great political difficulties. After all, these beneficiaries would feel, whether they needed the income or not, they did pay their social security taxes during all of their working years, with the assurance of a lifelong annuity once they retired, irrespective of their wealth and income. But taxing social security benefits, as recommended above, would in part accomplish the same thing, since the poor pay little or no taxes while the wealthy are taxed at higher rates. (Just as an interesting sideline aimed at those who for years have urged our government to tax less and spend less: We could accommodate them by rescinding taxation of social security benefits altogether and, instead, lowering monthly payments to those formerly taxed. This would not only reduce taxes and expenditures, it would also keep the money in the Social Security Fund; but unfortunately, it would involve diligent and costly scrutiny of the income levels of all social security recipients. Notice also, if you will, that as long as government appropriates these taxes for general expenditures, it also overstates actual annual social security disbursement since it simply takes back some of the money paid out to recipients.) Finally, President Clinton's proposal to commit 62 percent of the 1998 budget surplus, and similar percentages of future surpluses, to social security until the program is on a sound footing—a proposal backed in essence by Senate Republicans also—would be helpful, especially if budget surpluses continue for a number of years.

Still, using surpluses alone would not be enough; at best it would keep social security solvent for another decade or two. Several combinations of the steps suggested above, on the other hand, could easily protect social security for a century or longer; and they would not necessarily have to be enacted immediately, as long as they are in effect before the second decade of the twenty-first century when we would have to start dipping into the Social Security Fund. In any case, a well-thought-out program *must* be in place before the Fund becomes depleted around 2034.

A recent proposal to annul or greatly reduce cost of living increases, however, is another matter. While taxing social security incomes does not detrimentally affect non-taxpaying, low-income beneficiaries, not raising benefits as prices rise would place great hardships on those who can barely manage with what they have now. In 1989, our senators and congressmen did not hesitate to pass a law giving themselves annual salary increases tied to pay boosts that other federal employees receive. No wonder those who would like to see cost of living increases reduced feel uncomfortable to suggest it simply as a money-saving, budget-balancing measure. Hence, they came up with a new rationale: maybe we have been computing the inflation index wrong all along; maybe prices have not really been rising as fast as we have assumed, and we have therefore overstated increases in the "true" cost of living and meted out unreasonably and undeservedly high annual cost of living adjustments. Let's see then how we have been computing the inflation index over the years, and whether there is really something fundamentally wrong with it.

The CPI—the consumer price index—is published monthly by the Bureau of Labor Statistics of the U.S. Department of Labor. To compute it, 90,000 prices are checked each month in seven groups: food, housing, clothing, transportation, medical care, entertainment, and "other." From these prices, the cost of a "market basket" is put together on the basis of estimates as to how much of each product an average family buys—how much milk per month, how much car insurance, how many stamps, how many movie tickets—and a difficult chore this is. Say you check the price of a blouse in February: $29.95. You come back in March, but the spring merchandise has arrived, that blouse is no longer available, and others range in price from $14.99 to $89.99. So what happened to the price of ladies' blouses? Not easy to put together a "true" price index, is it? Moreover, as new products come into the market, "market baskets" do change (until 1940, for instance, the CPI reflected costs of trolley car fares but not automobiles). Therefore, once every 10 years, buying habits are surveyed and weights (how much of each item consumers actually buy) are assigned to goods in each of the seven consumer good categories mentioned above. This is the way we have been doing it for the past 80 years, since the days of World War I when the CPI was first conceived. This is the basis on which we decide annual cost of living increases not only for social security recipients but also for others such as workers who have indexed (meaning tied to the CPI) labor contracts. Even our income tax brackets are indexed so as to assure that we do not pay higher taxes on income increases that reflect nothing more than higher price levels. But could we have done it all wrong for all these years? Could we have computed our price increases mistakenly high all along?

To fund a research project that could, perhaps, come up with cost-saving reductions in the CPI, Congress set up a five-member Advisory Commission on the Consumer Price Index. Headed by Michael J. Boskin, an economics professor at Stanford University and a former chief of the White House Council of Economic Affairs under President Bush, the Advisory Commission released its report in December 1996: the CPI is being overstated by 1.1% annually.

If officially accepted, the cumulative effect of the reduction in cost of living increases would be disastrous for the millions of social security recipients for whom their monthly social security check provides the only or the major source of income. Boskin stated that when compounded over 12 years, the cumulative effect would lower the national debt by $1 trillion from what it would have been otherwise. One trillion dollars over 12 years! Can we even begin to grasp the hardship this would cause to many social security recipients, not to speak of millions of workers whose contracts are also indexed? It surely behooves us to ask whether the Advisory Commission was right when it charged that our consumer price index has been overstated for decades.

Their conclusion is based on many considerations. As just one example, the current consumer price index, they say, fails to reflect that consumers buy large quantities of items, whether Coca-Cola, Ivory Soap, toilet paper, or what have you, when these items are on sale. Granted, they may have a point, but that can hardly have much of an impact on the price index. Such goods and services as rent, penicillin, and dentures are not usually on sale. In any case, over half of the CPI's price overstatements are attributed to alleged failures to take quality improvements into consideration. In other words, if a Chevrolet today is twice as good as it was 10 years ago and it costs twice as much, there has been no change in price, the Advisory Commission tells us.

But to begin with, even a team of first-rate psychologists would find it impossible to conclude rates of satisfaction. How much better is an electric typewriter than a manual one? Twice as good? Three times as good? Let's suppose that over a number of years prices have doubled, but the "experts" decide that the quality of goods has doubled also. Well, then, so the argument goes, there has not really been a change in the "true" price index. But here is the trouble with this kind of approach: if, on the basis of such an evaluation no cost of living increases are granted, then social security recipients and others don't get enough money to buy the new goods, so they'll have to make do with manual instead of electric typewriters, tapes instead of CDs (not to speak of computers,) and forget about cat scans or MRIs. Or suppose these experts judge a college education today to be three times as good as it was 15 or 20 years ago (I can't fathom how they would arrive at "three times as good," but for that new CPI they would have to determine quality improvement indexes) and that it also costs three times as much, then in this respect, the new calculation would not allow for a change in the price index; however, that does not alter the fact that today's students will still have to pay three times as much in tuition. No wonder Katherine Adams refers to such questionable methods as "thought experiments that have no hard facts to back them."

If you were to assume that such considerations bother those who are sold on reducing the consumer price index you would be wrong. So, for instance, Alan Greenspan, chairman of the Board of Governors of the Federal Reserve System, went before Congress in January and again in March 1997, explaining that he favored a reduction in the CPI because it would greatly reduce monthly social security payouts, especially when the baby boomers reach retirement age. Well then, have we been all wrong over these past 80 years or is this merely another attempt to save money, irrespective of what it does to those who can least afford it? This author, for one, will not subscribe to such a "revised" consumer price index, even if it does save Uncle Sam a trillion dollars over 12 years. However, a Congress bent on balancing the budget and keeping it balanced at all costs is likely to trim cost of living increases somewhat, if not by the full 1.1 percent. Let's face it: adjusting for quality, "satisfaction," and the like is simply a device for achieving a desired outcome that you have in mind before you start.

Now a new idea seems to have gotten hold in Washington: "privatizing" part or all of social security, they call it. Although the idea has been around for a while, the issue gained credence when a 13-member Advisory Council on Social Security, appointed by President Clinton's Secretary of Health and Human Services Donna E. Shalala, in June 1994, came out with its report in January 1997. The 752-page, two-volume opus is so complicated, so technical, so jargon-laden that it makes your average computer instruction manual look like a first-grade primer.

All members agreed that at least part of social security contributions should be invested in the stock market which traditionally yields higher returns than government securities; but they disagreed as to the level of risk acceptable. The five most radical would replace the current social security system with mandatory individual savings accounts, employees themselves would decide what to invest their money in, and at retirement age these accounts would be converted into annuities. Six members of the panel opted for keeping the current system essentially as is, but they wanted to shore it up by having the government invest up to 40 percent in the stock market. Two members voted for a hybrid system, some combination of individual decision making with government management, supervision, and regulation. The precise details, if such a system were ever to be adopted, would have to be worked out at the congressional level.

The assumption underlying such proposals is that the stock market will continue to behave in the future as it has in the recent past, and what a flawed assumption that is. Throughout our history, we have had periods when the stock market dropped sharply; and it didn't always spring back quickly either. Stocks didn't regain their 1929 highs until 1954; and when stock prices declined drastically in 1973, it took almost 10 years for them to match the highs of January of that year. Betting that stock prices will keep rising rapidly because they did so in most of the 1980s and 1990s is like someone on Noah's ark projecting six more weeks of rain on the 39th day. When the stock market did drop drastically in the late summer of 1998—an event that had to come sooner or later—not a single voice could be heard anywhere about "privatizing" social security. The balances in the Social Security Trust Fund didn't flutter in the slightest; the Fund stood like a rock, undisturbed by the turbulence, the frantic trading, the uncertainty of the stock market. True, this time the stock market recovered quickly; but it went through disturbingly large up- and downswings thereafter. And as we should have learned from the past, a rapid recovery is by no means guaranteed. In any case, as the stock market turns bullish again, the issue of privatization of social security—supported and promoted by powerful special interests—is being raised once more.

If social security had been partially or fully privatized in 1998 when stocks dropped by almost 20 percent over a six-week period, what then? Millions of elderly retirees depend on their social security checks for their only or their major source of livelihood; they need a guaranteed, inflation-adjusted income. Would they, could they willingly consent to sudden reductions in their monthly checks, especially at times when a quick recovery is not in the offing? How would the government explain the intricacies of a dropping market to the widow of a former low-income worker who can barely make it on her monthly check as is? True, as the advocates of the proposed "privatization" of part or all of social security point out, over the long run, the stock market has always done well, and we can expect that it will continue to do so. But, as the British economist John Maynard Keynes put it so well over half a century ago, "in the long run we'll all be dead." What good does it do a poor elderly couple who can't pay the rent on their small apartment with their reduced check to know that five or ten years down the line, things will probably be so much better? Would elderly voters allow this to happen? I doubt it. If a stock market crash were to ravage their social security accounts, they would not be overly shy to demand a government bailout and the taxpayers would have to come up with the money. In practice, we could privatize only stock market profits, but losses would be socialized.

There is more. The purchase of all these stocks by itself will put the viability of the stock markets at risk. Depending upon which plan is adopted, between $1 and $4 trillion of payroll taxes would be put into the stock market between now and 2015. Such a huge increase in demand for stocks would obviously drive up stock prices (many say the stock market is already overvalued) and would therefore reduce—and probably reduce considerably—the return per dollar invested. (Dividends, after all, depend on the corporation's profitability; so, whether I sell you a share of General Motors stock for $50 or $75, the dividends will not change, but at the higher price you get less per dollar invested). This drop of returns on investment is the stuff that leads to stockholders panicking, selling off, and to the stock market crashing. And, when the downturn comes, we will not be able to stand by and do nothing. We had to bail out the Chrysler Corporation and the Savings and Loan Associations. For moral as well as for political reasons we cannot—and certainly should not—turn our backs on millions of retirees facing poverty in old age. Keeping money in government securities may be less profitable; but social security must remain secure. Risk taking may be a vital element of sound investing; it must not be allowed to be an element in old age security financing. And if it's not a good idea for the government to risk some of the Social Security Fund's holdings on the stock market, it's even worse to turn the decision making over to the contributors themselves. Individual workers, untrained in investment financing and subject to the selling techniques of skilled advertisers and promoters—well, you get the picture. But if you still think that government investing in the stock market may be the answer, think again. Would this not lead to a conflict of interest beyond anything we have ever experienced? Just think of the government holding hundreds of millions of dollars worth of stock in a corporation that runs into financial difficulties. Do you think that there would be an objective analysis to determine whether or not that company should be bailed out with taxpayers' money? Is this really how we want to run the social security system, how we want to run our country?

All that has been said above does not cover one final point, the phenomenal immediate cost of converting to such "privatization" of social security. The tens of billions of dollars that year after year have gone into the coffers of government (via the Social Security Fund and secured by government securities, to be redeemed at some later date) will now no longer be available. Watch out, budget balancers! You may have a problem of major proportions at hand. In any case, do Americans really want the government to be the largest holder of corporate stock in the world, to be a major stockholder in many private corporations, able to vote enormous blocks of stock at stockholders' meetings? Or do we want tens of millions of ill-prepared workers to play high-stake individual games of retirement roulette? "Letting the Social Security System invest in the stock market is a risky strategy," warned the investigative arm of Congress, the General Accounting Office, in April 1998. "It could be like a high-stakes poker game," said Marilyn Moon, Urban Institute economist and social security trustee. "Some beneficiaries could win big, but others could lose big."

While these proposals constitute an unprecedented, and in this author's view, uncalled for alteration in the way we finance social security, it should be emphasized that the Advisory Council also recommended in no uncertain terms that the essence of the social security system be kept intact: the continuation of the basic relationship between employee-employer contributions, universal participation providing benefits for all contributors, and the assured availability of benefits for future generations. Various members of the Council also urged consideration of steps mentioned before such as raising contributions, increasing maximum income levels on which they are collected, pushing up the retirement age,

and expanding the system to include state and local government employees. But it is their proposal of investing parts or all of social security
contributions in the private sector that overshadows all others and
threatens the very security in old age which the government has promised and Americans have rightly expected ever since 1935. It is on the
basis of this promise—really this guarantee—and with this expectation
in mind that they have made their mandatory social security contributions during all their working years.

Social security is not a failure; on the contrary, it has been and is our
government's greatest success. "Social security has changed literally
what it means to be old," said President Clinton. He is right, you know.
For over half a century it has been the mainstay of retirement income
for Americans. Economic security in old age is part of the American
dream, and it is social security that has made this dream a reality. Since
social security has been with us for over 60 years, young people have
little conception of life without government-sponsored old age pensions.
True, social security was never intended primarily as an assistance program for the needy. Yet, over the years it has saved tens of millions from
poverty; as recently as the 1950s, poverty rates among the elderly were
more than twice that of the population at large, but since 1985, poverty
among elderly in America has been no higher than among the rest of
the population for the first time in our country's history. Nearly two-
thirds of older Americans depend on social security for at least half of
their income and one in six has no other income. According to a recent
government release (*Budget of the United States, Fiscal Year 1999*), only 3
percent of married and 16 percent of single social security recipients fall
below the poverty line; but without social security, the report says, 41
percent of the former and 61 percent of the latter would live in poverty.
To cut benefits as a means to help balance the budget is to misplace our
priorities; to cut them so that we can lower the taxes of the well-to-do
is unconscionable.

Social security is not on the verge of bankruptcy either, and our children and grandchildren can rest assured that it will be there when they
retire. "The difficulty of balancing social security over the next 75 years
is being greatly exaggerated," says Robert M. Ball, former commissioner
of the Social Security Administration and a member of the Advisory
Council on Social Security. "There is no need to make major cuts in
promised benefits. . . . And certainly," he says, "there is no need to sub-
stitute uncertain returns from individual savings accounts for part of the
basic social security system. There is no need to panic." And Horace B.
Dees, executive director of the American Association of Retired People
agrees. "Social security" he says, "is not in crisis. There is no reason to
rush radical reform proposals that would undermine the stability of the

program." And he goes on to point out that channeling a part of payroll taxes into individual investment accounts would be "especially risky for poor and middle-income elderly who rely on social security" as the main source of their income.

Those senators and congressmen who would dismantle the current program, or failing that, would have Wall Street grab a piece of the action, don't pay social security taxes themselves. Just as our presidents and vice presidents, they have their own pension funds that guarantee them a secure old age at incomes several times that of even the highest social security beneficiaries. Have you ever heard any of them expressing concerns that they will not get their pensions, that the government will not be able to pay them their due when the time comes? Have you heard them express fear that *their* pension funds will go broke? It's not that they don't deserve their pensions, not that they shouldn't get them. Just let them not take ours away or gamble our "trust fund" on risky ventures.

Chapter 9

Welfare: Which Way Now?

The Constitution obligates us, "the People of the United States . . . (to) promote the General Welfare"; but our government in Washington failed to heed this directive for the first 150 years of our country's history. With but few exceptions, such as pensions for members of the armed forces who had completed their years of service, there was no effective federal welfare program in place; and the depression of the 1930s found the largely locally administered and locally financed social welfare provisions then in existence totally inadequate to cope with the needs of the millions of unemployed and poor. The free market had failed "to promote the general welfare," and government action was called for.

With countrywide support in the elections of 1932 and 1936, Roosevelt was able to insist on the enactment of a wide variety of social welfare legislation. In quick succession, the Congress established a number of agencies (the Public Works Administration, the Civil Conservation Corps, and numerous others) that made grants to the states for work relief and for direct cash relief, provided federal work camp jobs for millions and part-time jobs primarily for needy high school and university students; and it helped establish job training and counseling programs. Although only temporary in nature, most of them lasting only two to ten years, these programs had a lasting influence, for they paved the way for future use of public funds, administered by public agencies and aimed at providing training, work, and assistance (cash, housing, health care, etc.) for the needy.

And then, in August 1935, the crowning achievement: the Social Security Act that offered a measure of economic security for the elderly and eventually for their dependents, their survivors, the blind and the handicapped, and that also brought with it unemployment insurance and supplemented mothers' pensions with Aid to Dependent Children, later renamed Aid to Families with Dependent Children (AFDC). Four years thereafter, widows became eligible for social security benefits, AFDC began to serve primarily divorced, deserted, and unwed mothers, and it became by far the country's largest welfare program.

Administrations that followed continued the trend of the 1930s. The National School Lunch Program was started under Truman when Congress grew concerned about the number of military recruits who failed physicals due to nutrition-related problems. The program has been providing one-fourth, one-third, and more of the daily nutritional requirements for millions of children ever since. The Food Stamp program, introduced as a pilot project under Kennedy in 1961 and made permanent under Johnson in 1965, has proved of enormous value in the battle of millions of poor families against hunger. Lyndon Johnson's War on Poverty instituted education and training programs for the needy that lasted through the Reagan, Bush, and early Clinton years, and so did other "entitlements" (in other words, programs that provided aid automatically to qualified beneficiaries) established during the Nixon and Carter years that guaranteed minimum income for the poor. In 1974, the year Nixon resigned, Congress created SSI (Supplemental Security Income), a program that grants new benefits to the indigent elderly, blind, and disabled; and it set up "Legal Aid" that provides free legal services to the poor, not just in criminal cases but in civil suits also, such as when poor renters bring suit against their landlords—something they could never have afforded before, no matter how justified their claim. George Bush, in his 1988 campaign, pledged to request sufficient funding for important programs to reach young children, such as the school lunch program and the Women, Infant and Children (WIC) nutrition program that offers food assistance and nutrition screening to low-income pregnant women and their children up to age five. Once elected, he made good on his promise, asking for a 9 percent increase for WIC spending in his 1992 budget; and in his 1992 State of the Union Address, he called Head Start, unveiled in the mid-1960s under Nixon's presidency, "a program that helps children born into want move into excellence." Bob Dole, Senate Republican leader at that time, co-sponsored a bill asking for a $2 billion increase in financing WIC, Head Start, and the Job Corps, and he called these programs "the best weapons we have in our fight against poverty." (A 1990 study by the U.S. Department of Agriculture reported that for every dollar spent on WIC we save between $1.77 and $3.13 on Medicaid costs in just the first 60 days after birth). It seems we had not completely forgotten FDR's message to the 1938 Congress: "Government has a final responsibility," he said, "for the welfare of its citizens. If private cooperative efforts fail to provide work for willing hands and relief for the unfortunate, those suffering hardships through no fault of their own have a right to call upon the government for aid. And a government worthy of its name," he continued, "must make a fitting response."

Never in the history of mankind has there been a country more able to provide each and every inhabitant with sufficient food, shelter, clothing, medical care, education, and other necessities of life. But as the welfare rolls increased drastically, from 350,000 in 1940 to over 14 million AFDC recipients in the mid-1990s, attitudes among the rest of the population changed. Except for the upper 2 percent, most people had not been getting ahead for the last 25 years. No wonder that under the influence of the media and the politicians who overwhelmingly tend to reflect the views of the haves, rather than those of the voiceless have-nots, the public blames the poor and not the rich for our economic ills. Just listen to the current brand of welfare reformers and you get the impression that welfare is a threat to our whole way of life. Stereotypes are created of hardworking Americans, their hard-earned income taxed to support lazy, non-working, unmarried, teenage welfare mothers who have more and more children simply to collect more welfare money, and drunk or high-on-drugs men unwilling to get a job. Totally ignored, in these stereotype views, are the facts: True, out of wedlock children of teenage mothers have greatly increased in numbers; however, this is so not only among welfare recipients but also among the population at large, in the United States and to a lesser extent in the rest of the industrial world as well. Most of these mothers had work experience but their jobs didn't pay enough to take care of a family, not to speak of hiring babysitters—and anyhow, the majority of them stay on welfare for less than two years. Among mothers who receive food stamps, a December 1995 study funded by Rutgers University found, 77 percent work over 20 hours, and 55 percent over 36 hours per week. If their purpose is simply to have more children, how can we explain the fact that in the late 1960s one welfare mother in three had four or more children while that holds true for only one in ten today? And when the welfare bashers tell us that there is no need for anyone to be poor in our country since we have equal rights and equal opportunities for all, they remind me of Anatole France's often-cited dictum that "The law in its great majesty forbids the rich as well as the poor to sleep under bridges, to beg in the streets, or to steal bread." Sure, both the rich and the poor in our country have the right to buy a $3 million house in the Berkeley Hills, to purchase a Mercedes convertible, or to take a $10,000 cruise; but you and I know that's meaningless.

So, if it's hard for the present generation, do at least the children of the poor have the opportunity to ever get there? Not easily, for the road out of poverty is hard to find and even harder to travel. "Poverty breeds poverty," Lyndon Johnson said in his economic report to the nation in 1964. "Low incomes carry with them high risks of illness, limitations on mobility, limited access to education, information and training. Lack of motivation, hope and incentive is a more subtle but no less powerful barrier than lack of financial means. Thus the cruel legacy of poverty is passed from parents to children." We like "from log cabin to the White House" stories, but unfortunately, they are the exceptions rather than the rule.

True, there are some who cheat, who exploit the system, some even who take welfare from two or three states. But you would be hard-pressed to find any profession, any government or private agency, any corporation without its share of swindlers, frauds, and crooks, and these need to be held fully accountable for their wrongdoings, be they white collar workers or welfare recipients. It is equally true that, especially in inner city slums, there is a "welfare class," a section of the population who have made welfare their way of life, and that's a serious problem. It'll take education and training, living-wage job opportunities, and patient social workers to help families overcome hopelessness and lethargy, and to give them a vision of a better future for them and their children. Make no mistake, this would be a long and slow process; but the alternative of throwing these people out unto the street and starving their children can't be the answer. Apart from any moral obligation to do better than that, this would inevitably lead to more crimes committed by desperate parents, teenagers, and homeless people who have given up; and it costs more to keep a single individual in jail than to have two or three families on welfare. Moreover, let's not blow it all out of proportion. We hear a lot about this stereotype of "undeserving" individuals taking advantage of the system. True, there are more than just a few, but they still constitute only a small minority of welfare recipients. Or do you really believe that most public assistance beneficiaries choose to be poor? That they could get off welfare if they just wanted to, although unemployment always numbers in the millions? That women go on having children just so they get a few more dollars in welfare and food stamps? That immigrants come to this country not to find a job but to get a free ride at taxpayer's expense? That its great fun to live on welfare? And do you really believe that we ought to deprive the deserving, and especially the children, of health care, food, a home, and a future because there are some who are taking advantage of the system?

But now, it seems, we are putting "an end to welfare as we know it." The federally dominated antipoverty safety net, carefully put in place by administration after administration since the days of Roosevelt's presidency, is being shredded. History's richest nation is rewriting its compact with the poor. After more than 60 years of promising to provide for mothers and children in need, America is declaring its experiment in public altruism a dismal failure and is telling its poor to take care of themselves. Because a chorus of political advisers told President Clinton that a veto would cost him the election, he signed a welfare reform bill on August 22, 1996 that revised radically our nation's welfare law, replacing a safety net with a tangle of rules and regulatory sanctions that will, for many, lead to an abyss—a welfare bill which 15 years earlier even the most ardent budget cutters would not have dared to propose. In the name of responsibility, they have devised a system that disqualifies many people, erases the entitlements of formerly eligible individuals to assistance, empowers states to reduce benefits levels, and introduces cuts affecting mostly the poor; and Clinton's post-election attempts to rescind some of the most Draconian cuts have since met with but very limited success in a Republican-dominated Congress. "People in the White House have only the flimsiest grasp of social reality," commented Senator Daniel Patrick Moynahan (D-NY), "thinking anything doable is equally undoable, as for example, the horror of this legislation." And even Senator Slade Gordon (R-WA), who called the bill "magnificent," admitted "it is not at all certain what the consequences will be."

The new welfare bill, tellingly entitled the "Personal Responsibility and Work Opportunity Act of 1996," effectively ends "entitlements," the federally guaranteed welfare benefits to the needy, and it replaces Aid to Families with Dependent Children (AFDC, the main cash welfare program since the Great Depression, now renamed Temporary Assistance to Needy Families—TANF) by block grants to the states. Within two years, able-bodied adults of working age must go to work or participate in job training or other job-related activities; and with but few exceptions, families may receive benefits for no more than five cumulative years during a lifetime. The law greatly tightens eligibility for food stamps, for supplemental security income for the aged, blind, and disabled, and the types of disabilities that qualify children for benefits. Moreover, legal immigrants, repeat *legal* immigrants, were denied virtually all welfare benefits unless they are veterans or have refugee status (although some of the benefits have been restored to them, as discussed on page 76). The law in its entirety practically abrogated federal commitment to the needy and gave states vast new authority to run their own welfare programs.

The primary impetus to reform "welfare as we know it" came from the proclaimed goal to "balance the budget by 2002," evidently on the backs of the most vulnerable in our society while giving substantial tax cuts to the middle, and even more to the uppermost income earners. While the new welfare bill entails huge cuts in many programs, its most important part is "workfare instead of welfare." Sounds so simple: active hands instead of handouts, paychecks instead of welfare checks. Who could dispute that physically and mentally capable welfare recipients of working age should get off their butts, get a job, and earn a living. But, unfortunately, it isn't all that easy.

It's not that the idea is new, that welfare-to-work programs don't exist. There are hundreds of them around our country. In 1996, job training programs served 650,000 people. But the scale envisioned now is something else again and the problems facing the project are formidable.

Just for a starter, there aren't enough jobs for all the able-bodied welfare recipients of working age, not to speak of jobs that pay a living wage. (In 1979, a minimum wage job enabled a full-time worker to support a family of three; but in 1999, even at the new minimum wage of $5.15 an hour, a mother with two children would still be well below the poverty level.) Keep in mind that few people on welfare have marketable skills that would enable them to land decently paying jobs; just about half of them are high school dropouts, untrained, unskilled, often functionally illiterate, unqualified for other than low-paying, dead-end employment. So, training programs for millions of prospective workers need to be funded. Merely asking welfare recipients to trade poverty on welfare for poverty at work, sending them out on minimum wage jobs that will not allow them to take care of themselves or their families and that will never let them rise even to lower middle-class status will not solve the problem. Until they can earn a living wage on their own, we may have to subsidize employers who hire workers off the welfare roles, and subsidize workers in the form of food stamps and housing allowances.

Second, many of the jobs available do not carry health care coverage. Since these workers are unable to pay for health insurance themselves, we either must insist that employers provide it (which would make it less likely that they'd hire them at all) or we must continue providing it for them, as we do when they are on welfare until they reach a certain income level, or get a job that offers health care benefits.

Next, how about daycare? Two thirds of TANF (formerly AFDC) recipients are children, too young to go to work. Say a welfare mother gets a job. How about these children? Who will take care of them? Is "informal care" the solution, untrained welfare mothers keeping six or eight of them in a dilapidated, small apartment, serving them a daily 9:00–5:00 TV fare? That obviously can't be the answer. President Clinton's proposed 1997–1998 budget provided for $4 billion over six years for daycare; but by estimates of the Congressional Budget Office and most other non-partisan advisers, that's still at least $1 billion, or tens of thousands of children, short of what is needed.

Even just getting to the job and back can be a daunting project. The majority of welfare recipients have no, or at least not reliable, cars. Public transportation is not always available, especially outside of bigger cities, and where it is available, it is often prohibitively expensive for low-income earners (for instance, commuting from the Bay area in California across the bridge to a job in San Francisco can easily cost five dollars or more for a round trip, depending where you are travelling from, or more than $100 a month).

To begin to solve the problem, and in addition to health care coverage and to food and housing subsidies until the workers are able to earn a living wage on their own, we must be willing to provide pre-job training, daycare for the children, and transportation to and from the jobs (some communities have started doing just that, anywhere from financing car repairs, buying new batteries, providing vans and buses, helping people financially to move closer to their jobs, and in some cases, where necessary, buying used cars for them).

If we don't do all that, we will make it just about impossible for millions of welfare recipients to take and keep a job, if there is one available. Doing something about it, on the other hand, is not going to help the taxpayer save money right then and there. On the contrary, it would involve enormous expenditures at the outset (although they would not be quite as dreadful as depicted because they would be somewhat offset by decreasing welfare rolls and by increasing tax collections from some of the gainfully employed). But let's stop kidding ourselves: unless these steps are taken, we might as well forget the welfare-to-workfare idea altogether and either keep unemployed welfare beneficiaries and their children on the dole or let them shift for themselves, bereft of adequate food, clothing, shelter, or medical care.

Regrettably, if we do spend all that money and do all the things outlined above we still haven't solved the problem. You see, when we finally find jobs for all these welfare recipients without driving other workers from their jobs and into welfare, and without depriving temporarily unemployed not-on-welfare workers from finding jobs, our unemployment rate would drop dramatically, and that's the goal, isn't it? But, as pointed out before, THE FEDERAL RESERVE, FEARFUL OF INFLATION, IS NOT LIKELY TO ALLOW THIS TO HAPPEN. They'll raise interest rates, they'll raise bank reserve requirements, they'll sell government securities on the open market to take money out of circulation, they'll do anything they can to keep the economy from "overheating" and the unemployment rate from dropping below 4.5 percent. (Actually, 1999 was the first year in a long time that they allowed it to drop to 4.2 percent because there didn't seem to be any inflationary pressures in sight for the foreseeable future). Japan, for decades, was able to grow and prosper with unemployment rates of 2 percent and less; but if we are unwilling to change our economic mentality and not only accept but strive toward low rates of unemployment and keep inflation under control by different means, we might as well keep making payments to the unemployed and their families or simply abandon them altogether.

What the 1996 "welfare reform" bill did to legal immigrants is unconscionable—there is no other word for it—restricting for most of them access to dozens of federal programs including food stamps, medicaid, income for the old, the disabled, the blind. The 93-year-old Korean woman, living by herself, unable to become a citizen because she was too old to learn English when she came here and her son has died since; the young Italian couple, both working at McDonald's since he was "downsized" six months ago—here for only three years, not eligible for citizenship as yet, whose 14-year-old son wants to become an army pilot; the young woman from El Salvador, almost five years in this country, awaiting her citizenship papers, cleaning houses, who got into a car accident—they all were left to shift for themselves. "All our people, except full-blooded Indians," FDR once reminded us, "are immigrants or descendants of immigrants, including those who came here on the Mayflower." And the inscription on the Statue of Liberty, how could we forget: "Give me your tired, your poor, your huddled masses yearning to breathe free." We are talking about *legal* immigrants here, mind you, most of them American citizens of tomorrow. And let it be emphasized that, according to the Census Bureau, only some 5 percent of these legal immigrants of working age receive public assistance benefits, about the same percentage as working-age American citizens. President Clinton's efforts to rescind some of the most Draconian aspects of the 1996 Welfare Reform bill have met with limited success: by 1998, food stamps and some other benefits were restored to thousands of legal immigrants; but the House-Senate deal allocated less than one-third of the $2 billion President Clinton had asked for to cover up to 730,000 immigrants for the next five years.

All power to the states, the new welfare reform seems to say, as block grants relieve the federal government of responsibility for the needy. So, what's wrong with that? Can't the states do a better job, as we are assured they will? Perhaps they can, perhaps they can't, I don't know, I am not sure. But I *am* sure that we ought to have a *centralized* safety net for all, whether they happen to live in New Mexico, Kansas, or South Carolina. And that's what we are *not* going to get. Historically, and by tradition, different states have different attitudes toward social spending. In December 1996, for instance, before the law took effect, Vermont was the top spender on welfare. "We have a tradition of social responsibility," said Jane Kitchel, commissioner of Vermont's Department of Welfare. Rich but penny-pinching Texas, on the other hand, ranks forty-eighth among our 50 states in spending for social needs. "Texas," said Michael A. Jones, spokesman for the Texas Department of Human Services, "believes that too much aid breeds dependence and poverty." So, there is a huge range of welfare benefits, varying from $923 per month for a family of three in Alaska to $577 in New York City, to a low of $120 in Mississippi. There are, of course, cost of living differences among regions, but that alone does not account for the disparity. Living costs are similar in Georgia and Texas, but Georgia pays $92 a month more than Texas' measly $188. Some states pay adults to finish high school, others provide more daycare. Kentucky will truck families out of no-jobs Appalachia to Louisville or Lexington where there are more employment opportunities. But without at least some kind of mandatory, uniform safety net, the more generous states may become "welfare magnets," attracting the "huddled masses" from other, less charitably minded parts of the country.

While drastically slashing virtually all welfare programs—TANF, SSI, school lunch programs, food stamps, housing assistance, and what have you—there is one program that has so far not been touched: corporate welfare. Rarely mentioned and little known to the general public, we are subsidizing big business to the tune of more than *50 billion dollars* per year, a projected total of $265 billion over five years, from 1995 to the end of the century. You would be hard-pressed to find a single *Fortune* 500 company that is not subsidized annually with millions of dollars of taxpayers' money. Virtually all industries reap the benefits, fast food, aerospace, telecommunications, biotechnology, sugar, even tobacco growers. We own the public airways, but radio and TV stations pay pittances for their broadcasting licenses—and these licenses are literally worth billions of dollars. IBM, Dupont, McDonald's, Sunkist oranges, Gallo winery, and dozens of others get hundreds of millions to promote their products overseas. The Rural Electrification Administration subsidizes profitable electric utilities at the cost of some $2 billion a year. The Advanced Technology Program transfers millions of taxpayers' dollars to corporate giants like General Electric and Xerox. Cities that don't have enough money for schools, playgrounds, and city streets come up with hundreds of thousands if not millions of dollars to attract new industries and retail outlets.

Defenders of corporate welfare will tell you that these subsidies are needed to promote exports and to create jobs in the cities. But don't you think that there is something wrong with a system that cuts food stamps, housing allowances, and school lunches from the needy and turns the savings over to giant corporations who earn and distribute to their owners profits into the hundreds of millions of dollars per year and who, according to the philosophy of a free enterprise system that they so strongly espouse, should not invite government subsidies but fend on their own in a free market. And as to creating employment in the cities: sure, the way the game is played today, cities have to compete with each other. But if none of them did, if there were a law preventing them from giving discriminatory tax breaks and subsidies to private businesses, would the new industries and retail outlets not have to locate in one city or another anyhow? True, in 1997 there was talk in the halls of Congress of a bipartisan attack on corporate welfare; but with many tens of millions of dollars funnelled by special interests into congressional campaign funds at every election, it is not too likely that corporate welfare will be on the table for more than inconsequential reductions.

The old social welfare programs haven't worked, we are told. Really now! Tell it to the elderly who no longer have to live in poverty; tell it to the mothers of children who no longer have to face hunger on the streets; tell it to the preschoolers in Headstart who, without it, would not get this early preparation for life; tell it to the children of the poor who daily enjoy a wholesome lunch in school; tell it to the handicapped who are no longer left to shift for themselves. No, the great social programs of the past were not the whims of liberal social engineers. To say this is to distort in an unconscionable way what really took place during the Great Depression and what has taken place since. In the days of old there were no welfare chiselers because there was no welfare—or unemployment insurance, or social security. If you couldn't find a job or were too old to work, you lived off your savings if you were lucky enough to have any, or off your relatives if they could afford it, or off private charity if you could get it, or you stood on street corners selling apples or begging, and you made it somehow—or you didn't.

When they keep telling us how much better it used to be before all these government handouts, before the days of the "welfare mess," when they suggest nostalgically that we return to the "good old days" of yesteryear, one cannot help but wonder what they are talking about. Return to what? To the days of slavery? To the sweatshop conditions in northern textile mills where illiterate children worked 10 to 12 hours a day, six days a week and parents longer than that? To the days when one out of every three Americans willing and able to work couldn't find a job and there was no unemployment compensation or government aid for the destitute (nor, for that matter, for the old, the sick, or the handicapped)?

Of those who are all too ready to destroy any vestiges of the federal government's obligation to protect the most vulnerable among us, many come from wealthy homes. "Too many in Congress," charges Ohio governor George Voinovich, "simply haven't a clue what it's really like to be poor in our country." All too true, but there are others who in their own lives have taken full advantage of the system they are now ready to do away with. As just one example, take Phil Gramm, senator from Texas, one of the most ardent protagonists of huge cuts in all entitlement programs who admonished us that if we stay on the old course, "in 20 years we're not going to be living in the same country." But interestingly, when he was born his father was supporting the family on a veterans' disability pension, he went to the University of Georgia with his tuition and expenses taken care of by the government under the War Orphans Act, and his graduate work was paid for again by the government under the National Defense Education Act—all three "entitlement" programs.

The suggestion, finally, that religious congregations and volunteer organizations absorb the cuts in federal programs borders on the absurd. If that kind of nineteenth-century system of private welfare had worked, twentieth-century welfare would not have been invented. We are talking here of tens of millions of people in need and of many tens of billions of dollars. The very most we can expect churches and charities to do is to supplement government efforts. Equally absurd and simply untrue is the idea that if we just lower the taxes of the wealthy, they'll contribute more to charities. New Hampshire has no sales or state income taxes, but in donations to charities it ranks fiftieth among our states.

The bill passed by Congress and signed into law by President Clinton in August 1996, a bill that camouflaged budget cuts as "welfare reforms," is a recipe for a catastrophe in the making. Eight million families with children, many working poor with food stamps, will lose an average of $1,300 a year; and 2.6 million additional Americans—one million of them children—will likely sink into poverty. Hardships for legal immigrants started in mid-1997 when the law went into effect (although some benefits have been restored since, as discussed above); for the rest of America's poor, the big hit will come in a few years. A two-year "get-a-job" time limit that disregards the job market, a lifetime five-year welfare limit no matter how the economy performs will spell disaster. Even a regretful President Clinton seemed to realize it when, in a talk to a political congregation at the National Prayer Breakfast in the Washington Hilton Hotel in February 1997, he had this to say about welfare: "We didn't change it; we tore it down; we threw it away."

It's time to realize that welfare is not responsible for our economic ills, that to reform it properly and not just abandon the poor—to make it "an opportunity, not a life style," as President Clinton put it—will cost money, not save us money, for a while at least, as discussed above; money for job training leading to jobs that pay a living wage, for temporary food stamps and housing allowances where necessary, for child care, for transportation so workers can get to their jobs, for health care coverage for them and their children, and for a safety net when there are no jobs available—for a safety net also for those too old or otherwise physically or mentally unable to meet work requirements; we can hardly let them fall by the wayside, unattended and uncared for.

Let's face it: we are far behind most industrialized nations in providing social services for the needy. But our society like other humane societies, does have a responsibility to help meet the needs of those who cannot care for themselves, and especially the needs of young children. We must not allow our government to abrogate this responsibility. What we need is not so much "an end to welfare as we know it;" but rather, "an end to poverty as we know it."

Chapter 10

Health Care: A Social Responsibility or a Profitable Business?

Is there a health care crisis in the United States? That depends on where you put your stethoscope. If you have adequate health care insurance and money to cover deductibles, copayments, and out-of-pocket expenses for medicines and procedures not covered under your plan, you can get the best care available anywhere. If you don't, that's quite a different matter.

We have the world's best health care system, we are told. We surely spend more on health care—more in total dollars (well over a trillion dollars in 1999), more as percentage of GDP than any other country in the world (almost 15 percent), twice as much per person (over $4,000) as Germany or Japan. So why are we so far down on the totem pole? Why is our life expectancy shorter and our infant mortality rate considerably higher than that of Canada, Japan, Australia, or Western Europe, including Italy and Spain? The answer is simple: it's that darn average again. It's not the residents of Malibu, California or Coral Gables, Florida, who experience the high mortality rates; it's not the children who are born and raised in affluent suburbs and who have the best of care that die in unduly large numbers in infancy. It's the lower-income earners, the *43 million Americans* without health insurance of any kind that pull the average down. The sons and daughters of the rich and famous may perhaps be more prone to acne and allergies; but it's the children who have to manage without the necessary doctors' visits, tests, treatments, and medications, usually with less than adequate prenatal care and without standard vaccinations, who are more likely to be in what so tellingly is called "poor" health, more likely therefore to die at an early age. (A recent study, published in the June 3, 1998 issue of the *Journal of the*

American Medical Association, gives the death rate of Americans with an annual income below $10,000 as more than three times that of people making $30,000 or more.)

The uninsured are not the elderly or people with disabilities; they may not be adequately covered under Medicare, but only 1 percent of them is without any health insurance at all. Nor is it the utterly poor, the ones without any assets to speak of; they are at least partially covered under Medicaid, the federal-state program that provides health care for the indigent. It's mostly the working poor and their families (one-third of the uninsured are children), the ones not covered on their jobs, who barely earn enough to make ends meet, can't afford their own health insurance, but are not eligible for Medicaid because their income is "too high."

As did Roosevelt, Truman, and Nixon before him, Clinton tried to get universal health care coverage for all Americans. "If you send me legislation that does not guarantee every American private health insurance that can never be taken away, you will force me to veto the legislation," he said in his January 1994 State of the Union Address. He gave Congress an all-or-nothing choice. Under the pressure of special interests in the health care industry, and in spite of the word "private" in his statement that assured the continuance of private health insurance, the Congress refused to even consider such universal coverage, but coverage was expanded. Under the 1997 budget accord, the federal government is providing $24 billion to the states over a five-year period, hopefully to cover "up to five million" of the 14 million uninsured children. Unfortunately, these few-strings-attached block grants to the states are bound to result in a hodgepodge of programs with different eligibility standards and benefit packages; and the government has nothing in the works for the majority of the uninsured, the adults, 23 million of them employed. Still, this effort, inadequate as it may be, is at least a step in the direction of greater health care coverage for needy children.

Until a few years ago, only two among the 62 most industrialized countries in the world had no programs of guaranteed health care for all their citizens: the Union of South Africa and the United States of America. In May 1996, South Africa adopted a new Constitution guaranteeing water, food, housing, education, and *health care* for all. Now we are the only country left. Why?

"It would be really nice to have health care for all, but we can't afford it," seems to be the general attitude. Finland can afford it. Spain can afford it. Bulgaria can afford it. Costa Rica can afford it. We can't? Our government spends more than twice as much on the military than on health care. Yet, our three major diseases—cardiovascular disease, cancer, and chronic obstructive pulmonary disease—kill more Americans each and every year than have been killed in all the wars in our country's history. There always seems to be enough money for new and improved weapons of destruction—at times Congress allocates even more for military expenditures than the generals ask for. But when it comes to health care, government expenditures are inadequate, and to supplement them we have to rely on charities, on annual door-to-door collections, and on mail appeals to gather contributions for the fight against cancer, diabetes, multiple sclerosis, and other diseases that plague us.

The improvement of public health calls for better financing of currently starved research activities to discover and combat environmental, occupational, and social causes of diseases. Our history in that area is spotted, to put it mildly. As compared with European experience, our national health involvement came later and has been marked by stop-and-go endeavors. Under the Tenth Amendment to the Constitution, "the powers not delegated to the United States by the Constitution nor prohibited by it to the states are reserved to the states respectively, or to the people." Since there is no constitutional mandate for the federal government to provide health care, much of it has always been left to the states. Hence, such important advances in public health as chlorinization of water, pasteurization of milk, or child immunization programs were pioneered by individual states—and even today, without a national mandate, there are millions of children under age five in the United States who are not inoculated against major diseases.

Indeed, public health at the national level has been a stepchild in the competition for financial resources. The United States Public Health Service (USPHS), theoretically our number one public health agency, and its subdivisions, the National Institute of Health (NIH) and the Center for Disease Control (CDC), are hampered by traditional, constitutional state-versus-federal government limitations. The bulk of preventive services remains with state and local health departments, and much-needed funds at the federal level are cut instead of increased to meet rising needs. Apart from human considerations, why don't senators and congressmen realize how much current investments in medical research could save in terms of future medical expenditures? Surely anyone ought to see that scrimping on current funds and resources that would help us be better prepared for the spread of AIDS, the occurrence of legionnaire's disease, or even the slow return of TB are ill conceived. But let us now turn from the problem of financing medical research to our present and rapidly changing health care system and see how it and the changes to come affect various groups of our population and our society at large.

In recent years, those Americans who carry health insurance have been faced with rapidly increasing insurance premiums (often paid for by their employer), high deductibles (amounts they have to pay out of their own pocket before the insurance kicks in), and rising copayments (share of total medical expenses charged to insurance holders). No wonder individuals and business firms offering health insurance to their employees began to look for lower-cost health coverage; and investors found a new "business" to invest in: for-profit HMOs (health maintenance organizations) and similar for-profit managed health care plans.

Under the traditional fee-for-service system, doctors are paid for services performed. HMOs generally operate differently: while no two HMOs are alike (some have physicians on salary, some provide discounted doctors' fees, and they all vary in premiums charged and services offered to enrollees), the trend is definitely toward paying doctors a flat fee per subscriber per year ("capitation" is the official HMO term for this arrangement); and over half of all physicians associated with HMOs are already operating on that basis. In these cases, the physicians or groups of physicians pay part of all treatment costs they order; the rest of expenses covered under the HMO plan are usually paid for by the HMO out of a risk fund set aside for such purposes.

Under these circumstances, it is obvious that physicians and managed care organizations make more money if they treat less. Every referral to a high-cost specialist, every test, every operation, every use of sophisticated equipment, every hospital stay is a cost to them. It can come as no surprise that they welcome young and healthy enrollees, and would be happy to do without the elderly, and especially without the chronically ill elderly. No wonder HMOs generally offer doctors substantial bonuses for keeping costs down, and many have disassociated themselves from physicians who spend too much per patient. Even beyond that, AMA (American Medical Association) trustee Ted Lewers lets it be known that "HMOs often drop doctors who tell their patients about diagnostic tests and treatment options or who challenge the HMO hierarchy," but, he says, doctors are ethically bound to ignore such "gag rules." President Clinton called these don't-tell orders "unacceptable," and Vice President Gore charged that "for too many doctors, strict rules imposed by health plans have been turning the Hippocratic oath into a vow of silence." A December 1997 article in the prestigious *Journal of the American Medical Association*, drafted by the Ad Hoc Committee to Defend Healthcare and cosigned by over 2,250 Massachusetts doctors, nurses, and other health care professionals, asserts that the rise of managed care is threatening the soul of American medicine. "Canons of commerce are displacing dictates of healing, trampling our profession's most sacred values," the article says. "Physicians and nurses are being prodded by threats and bribes to abdicate allegiance to patients, and to shun the sickest who may be unprofitable."

In the case of Medicare patients, the government pays the HMOs a flat sum per enrollee—and the HMOs' financial incentive to reduce care, and the subsequent results, are obvious. A study published in the October 1996 *Journal of the American Medical Association* found that among chronically ill elderly patients aged 65 and over, declines in physical health were almost twice as common in HMO than in fee-for-service plan patients. Everyone ought to exercise care before deciding to enroll in an HMO or, for that matter, in any other health insurance plan (however, some enrollees don't have much choice if their employer offers only one health care plan). But as to senior citizens, and to chronically ill senior citizens in particular, unless money is the primary consideration and the cost of a medigap (Medicare-supplementary) policy is completely out of reach, they are especially well-advised to question the glittering advertisement, produced by Medicare HMOs, and to carefully evaluate their health needs. Over half of all Americans—and especially those without current medical problems—have already joined HMOs; but, understandably, only some 13 percent of the Medicare population have opted to do so.

In the early days, the first HMOs were not run for profit; the California-based huge Kaiser Permanente, for instance, is still operated on a not-for-profit basis. But nowadays, we witness a definite trend toward for-profit organizations in the managed health care field (from 1988 to 1994, enrollment in them just about doubled, while not-for-profit HMOs experienced only a 25 percent increase in membership.) And the first duty of for-profit HMOs is clearly toward the shareholders, the investors, and not the patients. Administrators, often non-medical personnel, make decisions guided not by the patients' interest but by profits. And that is unfortunate. "No patient should have to wonder if their doctor's decision is based on sound medicine or on financial incentives," said Clinton's Health and Human Services Secretary Donna Shalala.

Virtually all HMOs limit subscribers' choice to doctors and hospitals associated with them. Patients selecting outside doctors and care facilities will either be charged substantially higher copayments or will find that such services are not covered at all. And physicians in the managed care field are faced with some 1,800 guidelines that tell them how they are to proceed with treatments. Public outcries resulted when doctors began to go through with some of the most extreme directives such as "drive-through deliveries" that allow a new mother only one night in the hospital, or outpatient mastectomies that force women who have undergone such a drastic procedure to change their bandages and clean the wound at home the very day of the surgery. President Clinton called such guidelines "dangerous and demeaning;" Senator Edward Kennedy commented that many managed care firms "have decided that the shortest route to higher profits and a competitive edge is by denying patients the care they deserve," and bills are popping up in Washington—some already enacted into law—to prevent women being discharged from hospitals prematurely after giving birth or undergoing mastectomies, mandating health insurers to allow legitimate emergency room visits

without prior authorization, and mandating them to cover certain sur-
gical procedures and medical treatments. But such piecemeal legislation,
necessary as it is at the moment, doesn't address the real problem: cost
and profit-driven health care that has been developing rapidly in our
country. With Americans increasingly concerned that managed-care
plans are controlling costs by short-changing quality of care, such organizations as the AARP are expressing hope that Congress will enact
bipartisan legislation which would set enforceable quality standards and
effective consumer protection. The Clinton administration has been
pushing for a "Patient's Bill of Rights" that would give sick people access
to specialists, access to emergency services, a choice of providers, and
the right to appeal decisions made by their health insurance providers.
In the first half of 1988 alone, insurance companies and their allies spent
$60 million to lobby against such new regulations ($112,000 for every
lawmaker, and that does not include campaingn contributions or expenditures for advertising); and by the end of 1998, Congress, busy with the
Monica Lewinsky affair and the impeachment of the President, had not
acted on the bill nor on a much weaker Republican-proposed patient
protection bill either. So in his 1999 State of the Union address, President
Clinton repeated his appeal to Congress to enact a comprehensive Patient
Bill of Rights.

In recent years, business has begun to intrude into all formerly largely
public health care services in the United States. Today, we can find
investor-owned, for-profit hospitals, clinics, orphanages, and even up-to-
now mostly volunteer-staffed hospices.

Although the great majority of our 5,200 hospitals are still not-for-
profit institutions, 700 have in the last ten years been turned into for-
profit business enterprises, and the number is growing. The largest,
ever-expanding Columbia, is a good example of how such organizations
operate. Started in 1986 by a lawyer, Richard Scott, who had never run
a hospital and had no training in medical management, Columbia HCA
(Hospital Corporation of America) grew within a decade from its humble
beginning to a $25-billion enterprise. It owns, by now, over 350 hospitals,
550 health care offices, and scores of other medical businesses in 38
states. With its 285,000 employees and 75,000 affiliated physicians, it is
by far the world's largest health care company.

The commonly held notion, engendered by extensive advertising cam-
paigns, that for-profit hospitals are highly efficient is a myth. In 1994,
administrative costs consumed 34 percent of the budget of for-profit hospitals, as compared with 24.5 percent of not-for-profit hospitals and 22.9
percent of public facilities (and, by the way, 10 percent of Canada's
government-operated single-payer system). Yet, for-profit hospitals consistently produce high profits for their owners. How do they accomplish
this feat? It's elementary. They cut hospital staff, including nurses (they

have 17 percent fewer employees, on the average, than their not-for-profit counterparts). They drastically reduce training periods (in one reported case from the normal six months to two weeks at Columbia). They focus on patients who carry insurance or can pay (and send others to the nearest community hospital, whenever possible), and, once established in a community, they raise charges to patients and insurance companies. According to a *New York Times* study, Columbia's regular median charges for a hospital stay are 35 percent higher per patient than the industry norm.

As an incentive, administrators are paid high bonuses (sometimes over 80 percent of their salaries and more than twice the average bonus not-for-profit hospitals pay) for "good performance." But while bonuses in not-for-profit hospitals are heavily weighted toward such achievements as providing better patient care, establishing programs that benefit the community, and lowering death rates, 90 percent of bonuses paid by Columbia and other for-profit hospitals are based on *financial* performance (and as to the other, discretionary, 10 percent, the company suggests that this be based on revenue-producing yardsticks like "growth in admissions and in surgery cases.") No wonder that so many of Columbia's practices have begun to anger employees, labor unions, consumer groups, and the general public. And courts and legislators have started to act. In Louisville, KY, a court ruled that Columbia's refusal to negotiate with a nurses' union violated federal law. In Rhode Island, the state Health Commissioner put on hold Columbia's purchase of the Roger William Medical Center in Providence. In Lawrence, KS, the city commission voted unanimously to deny Columbia a permit to build a for-profit hospital that would threaten the survival of the local community hospital which serves everyone, regardless of ability to pay—a decision likely to be nullified by the courts. In Michigan and California, the attorneys general rejected major Columbia hospital deals in Lansing and San Diego. From one end of the country to the other, communities have begun resisting Columbia's attempts to buy or destroy local community hospitals.

On top of this, the company has been the subject of several federal inquiries. Criminal investigators have been interviewing doctors, nurses, and others familiar with the company's practices around the country. And the federal agency that runs Medicare has been looking into charges that certain Columbia hospitals have systematically overbilled the government by overstating the severity of illnesses they treat. Amid a massive federal investigation, Columbia's founder and chairman Richard Scott and number two executive David Vandewater resigned in July 1997 (denying any wrongdoing.) Health care analysts say that the Columbia scandals will accelerate a reassessment of the free market approach to medicine.

So some steps toward controlling excesses have been taken at the local, state, and federal levels. There is even a 1986 federal law on the books requiring hospitals to examine and stabilize patients with "emergency medical conditions." But much more needs to be done. Would it not be reasonable to expect that any insurance policy spell out clearly which procedures are not covered because they are deemed experimental; that doctors have the right—nay, even the obligation—to inform patients of any procedure available and discuss it without penalty; and that referrals, tests, medications, and length of hospital stay be determined by the attending physician according to needs in each case and not by general administrative guidelines? To achieve such goals and to protect the public from other practices detrimental to the patient, appropriate legislation needs to be passed at the *federal* level, if we want it applied equally throughout the land. But even if it were, and urgent as its passage may be, it's once again only a temporary bandaid.

The fundamental problem that needs to be addressed sooner or later boils down to this: Do we really want doctors to be beholden to for-profit organizations whose primary goal is not the care of patients but the amassing of dividends for the investors? Should health care be a commercial product, sold like cars and television sets, with prices raised whenever the market will bear it, and with profit maximization the ultimate goal? Or should all Americans have a right to at least a minimum of health care as they do to education, to police and fire protection? As people do in every other industrialized country in the world? As do our legislators in Washington who have terrific health care benefits at very reasonable prices (the government picks up an average of 72 percent of the tab) but who vote consistently against guaranteeing it for the rest of us? As do all our 800,000 inmates in our prisons?

So far, the major protecting role our government has taken in the health care field is limited to protection for the elderly, for people with disabilities, and for the indigent—Medicare and Medicaid.

Enacted in 1965, Medicare—the nation's health commitment to the elderly and to people with handicaps—became the most important addition to the Social Security Act of 1935. More than half of the elderly over 65 had no insurance then and many of the rest were very inadequately covered. With at least limited medical care available to them since then, the health of our senior citizens and their life expectancy have increased dramatically.

Medicare consists of two parts. At age 65, every social security recipient is automatically enrolled in Part A, Medicare's hospitalization plan, and so are people with disabilities severe enough to make them eligible. This part of the Medicare program is financed in its entirety through a trust fund that depends on a special 1.45 percent tax levied on employees' salaries and matched by the employer. And at age 65 every social security recipient can also choose to enroll in Medicare's Part B, an insurance plan covering doctors' services and outpatient procedures. Participants in that program pay a fixed monthly premium, $45.50 in 1999, and the rest is financed out of general tax collections.

If you are on Medicare, you'll quickly discover that it pays only for about half of your medical expenses. Not covered, for instance, are prescription medicines unless you are a patient in a hospital (although in 1999 President Clinton asked Congress to legislate Medicare coverage of prescription medicines), routine eye examinations, routine physicals, and other screening services except for mammograms and pap smears, most charges for dental care and dentures, charges for hearing aids or routine hearing loss examinations, and many others. You also have no coverage if you travel outside the United States, except in certain instances in Canada and Mexico. As for other expenses, you'll have to pay the first $100 deductible and then have copayments of 20 percent thereafter (50 percent for most outpatient mental health care). In 1999, you also pay the first $764 of the first 60 days of hospitalization (these figures are raised every year), $191 a day thereafter up to the 90th day, $382 a day to the 150th day, and all hospital expenses after that. For skilled nursing facility care, Medicare covers only the first 20 days in full, you pay $95.50 a day up to 80 additional days, and all costs thereafter. And Medicare underwrites only a minute part (some $3 out of every $100) of regular, long-term nursing home care. Except for the indigent who are covered by Medicaid, the patients themselves are in most cases responsible for all of it. A 1998 AARP study shows that, not counting long-term-care expenses, the average Medicare recipients spend almost 20 percent of their income on out-of-pocket health care costs (35 percent for the poor, 17 percent for middle-income enrollees, but only 10 percent for those with incomes at least four times greater than the poverty level).

Obviously, elderly who depend only on Medicare are grossly underinsured. For all who can afford it, medigap plans, a kind of supplementary insurance, are available from numerous insurance companies, providing various coverage at various prices. For those unwilling or unable to take out this extra insurance, the average out-of-pocket expenses will run close to $3,000 a year. But as we already know, averages don't mean much; a senior citizen may discover that out-of-pocket expenses for medicines or for dental and hearing problems can easily add up to two or three times that much or more in a single year.

Another option available to Medicare beneficiaries is to sign up with one of the HMOs that has contracted with Medicare. In that case, the enrollee would pay a relatively low monthly premium and only nominal copayments. Outpatient medications and other services may be covered by the HMO also, but the risk that elderly subscribers in particular take when enrolling in an HMO have been discussed in detail above. And long-term nursing home care is not funded by medigap plans or by HMOs.

As of early 1999, the Hospital Insurance Trust Fund (Part A) had a surplus of $120 billion; yet it was in financial trouble. For the first time, in 1995, it started dipping into the reserves; and in the fiscal year 1996/ 1997, it spent over $9 billion more than it took in. Predictions then were that if nothing was done, the fund would run out of money by 2001; but high rates of economic growth and a $115 billion reduction in Medicare spending over five years, legislated under the 1997 budget accord, extended that date to 2010, allowing more time to deal with that quandary; and President Clinton's proposal to use 6 percent of the 1998 and of subsequent government budget surpluses to shore up the Medicare Trust Fund would presumably secure Medicare beyond the year 2020. The problem was and is, of course, rising costs.

In 1965, when Medicare was started, medicine was much more primitive than it is today. Heart surgery was rare, x-rays not MRIs were the state of the art. Nobody could foresee the advance in high-tech, high-cost medicine. Doctors' and hospital fees were just a fraction of what they are today and so were prescription medicines. Medicare expenses have been rising at 9 or 10 percent per year, three times as rapidly as our GDP and much faster than our overall rate of inflation. And it's not only the cost per enrollee, it's also the number of enrollees that has been increasing dramatically, and is expected to increase even faster in the future. With baby boomers, born between 1946 and 1964, well on their way toward senior citizenship, we are on the verge of a demographic tidal wave. The over-65 group now constitutes 14 percent, and by 2030 is expected to constitute 22 percent of our population. And the "oldest of the old," the over 85 group, is the fastest growing age group in our country. Obviously, something will need to be done to save Medicare.

Let's clarify one issue: it's Part A, Medicare's Hospital Trust Fund, that is in financial straits. As to Part B, it was expected that monthly premiums would cover half of all expenditures; but with rising costs and ever larger numbers of enrollees, they cover nowadays barely 25 percent. Actually, however, Part B is not in trouble. Why? Because unless we change the law or the government reneges on its guarantee, whatever is not collected in monthly contributions is simply paid out of the general tax fund. Premiums are deducted from the participants' monthly social security checks and are not put aside for any Medicare purposes, but rather added to the U.S. Treasury's general tax fund. They do not bolster in any way the Medicare Trust Fund. Therefore, recent proposals to greatly increase these monthly premiums "to preserve Medicare, to protect Medicare, and to strengthen Medicare," as then Speaker of the House Newt Gingrich put it in 1995, are misleading and simply not true. As a matter of fact, these monthly premiums have been raised every year, for instance from $42.50 in 1996 to $43.80 in 1998, and to $45.50 in 1999; and under the 1997 budget accord, they are to be raised gradually to $67 by 2002 (instead of $51.50 under the old law) which once again means shifting the burden of increased government expenditures onto the most vulnerable. Some 78 percent of Medicare enrollees earn less than $25,000 per year. In 1999, an elderly couple pays almost $1,100 per year for Part B Medicare benefits. To increase this to more than $1,600 over a period of three years will undoubtedly be a real hardship for many. It is in effect a special tax on the elderly at a time in which we are lowering taxes for the wealthy. (See more on this in Chapter 13 on taxes.) And it would do nothing to lighten the financial problem of Medicare's Hospital (Part A) Insurance Trust Fund.

But something must be done. Most legislators are in agreement that payments to physicians, hospitals, home care providers, and other health care agencies have to be reduced—and steps along these lines have already been taken to the displeasure of those affected. Regrettably, some doctors are even refusing to take Medicare patients. Of course, in any case, such pay-out reductions are no more than a very temporary step to delay the day of reckoning, and all advocates are aware of it.

Proposals have been afloat to charge higher monthly premiums to wealthy individuals and families on Medicare. While that would bring more money into the treasury without burdening financially those least able to afford it, it should be emphasized once again that this in no way improves the financial position of the Part A Hospital Insurance Fund.

A proposal by President Clinton to switch certain expenditures from Part A to Part B, referred to by opponents as merely a trick, is perhaps not much more than that. Still, under the 1997 budget accord, a portion of home-health spending was actually moved from Part A to Part B, a step that does shift the burden of these expenditures from a fund that is running out of money to the general tax fund—not a bad idea at that.

There are proposals to raise the age at which Medicare is available to the elderly from 65 to 67, surely not a step likely to improve the health of our senior citizens; the 1.45 percent health care tax levied on working people and matched by the employer will certainly be raised sooner or later; and Medicare beneficiaries, it has often been suggested, ought to join HMOs to reduce their out-of-pocket expenses—and as discussed above, Medicare in turn would pay the HMOs a fixed sum per month per patient; but so far, for obvious reasons, only one senior citizen in eight has opted for that solution.

Finally, as an alternative to standard health insurance, the idea of some kind of medical savings accounts has been advanced. Under the 1997 budget accord, a Medical Savings Account demonstration project was set up to include 390,000 beneficiaries. Medicare recipients who opt for this route would receive fixed monthly government payments that they would set aside in tax-free savings accounts to pay for medical expenses—a proposal originally vetoed by President Clinton in 1995. Such a choice may appeal to healthy senior citizens, but what would they do when they need, let us say, a $40,000 coronary bypass operation? Unless protected by a comprehensive government-underwritten safety net (which is not provided and which would run counter to the whole idea of individually managed medical savings accounts), they will have to carry additional, probably very expensive supplementary insurance, or most of them would have to spend down their holdings and join the ranks of the indigents on the Medicaid list—hardly a heartwarming proposal. And Medicare will surely be left to foot the bills of the sickest 10 percent of senior citizens who account for 70 percent of all Medicare outlays and who can hardly be expected to select a fixed monthly payment alternative.

It behooves us to listen ever so cautiously to those who would "save Medicare" by cutting it to the bone while advocating deep tax cuts for upper-income earners—especially if they and their ideological mentors in whose footsteps they follow are individuals long known to oppose government-sponsored social programs in general. When the debate over Medicare was on in the 1960s, the AMA (American Medical Association) hired Ronald Reagan to tell the American people that "one of these days you and I are going to spend our sunset years telling our children's children what it was once like in America, when men were free" (free not to have medical care, they must have meant). Bob Dole boasted in 1995 that he voted against Medicare 30 years before "because we knew it wouldn't work in 1965." So when his followers now seek to "preserve" it, how can we be sure they don't mean dismantle it? And, Senator Phil Gramm (R-TX) who in 1982 dismissed seniors' concerns about reduced social security benefits with the cold-hearted comment: "Most people don't have the luxury of living to be 80 years old, so it's hard for me to feel sorry for them," now poses as the savior of senior citizens. Is it not apparent that what these men really want is to reduce our nation's financial commitment to the medical care of our elderly and people with disabilities, and to most other social programs as well?

Medicaid is the government program that provides health care for some 35 million poor Americans. It's our country's health care safety net, "a lifeline, literally, for millions of children and families in America," Hilary Rodham Clinton called it. Once the cradle of Johnson's War on Poverty, it seems now headed for its grave, at least as a federal entitlement for all in desperate need.

Medicare has 37 million potential voters over 65, millions of others who soon expect to benefit from it, and the powerful 33 million-member (all over 55) AARP, the American Association of Retired People, to lobby for it in Washington and in state capitals. Medicaid is the program for the voiceless poor. No massive voting blocs, no powerful lobbyist to successfully plead its cause. Many Americans see it as nothing but a health program for promiscuous welfare mothers who would rather live on the dole than go to work, and for their children. But this stereotype doesn't fit the average recipients at all. In any case, there would be no need for Medicaid if we, like all other industrialized countries, had a universal health care program that covers everyone. And now, we are abandoning the formerly federal Medicaid program, replacing it by lump sum grants to the states with little if any strings attached. The health care of the most vulnerable—of senior citizens in nursing home facilities and of families with few assets and with income, if any, below the poverty line—is dumped on states with different proclivities, resolve, and financial ability to cope with the problem.

An estimated 43 percent of all elderly will spend some time in a nursing home, at current (and rising) costs of $25,000 to $50,000 a year. As stated above, Medicare underwrites only a minuscule portion (less than 3 percent) of long-term nursing home care. Regular health insurance plans generally don't pay for any of it, and special nursing home care policies don't give full coverage and are quite expensive, with premiums higher the later in life they are taken out. This surely is an area where a government-provided safety net is a necessity. A high percentage of elderly in nursing homes are people who don't have enough assets or income to meet the costs and Medicaid foots their bill. But Medicaid does not come in until virtually all the nursing home resident's finances have been wiped out. And that doesn't take too long. Half of all couples are impoverished within one year if one of them is admitted to a nursing home, although a spousal protection clause added to the Medicaid law in 1987 provides that a spouse can hold on to some assets such as a modest home and income—a provision some legislators on Capitol Hill now want to do away with, which would force a couple to spend itself into total poverty before making one of them eligible for Medicaid-paid nursing home care. Don't think either that you can get around that provision by turning your savings and possessions, accumulated over a lifetime, over to your children. If you were to do that and then at any time during the following five years go on Medicaid: well, since January 1997 that constitutes a criminal offense. And if you have spent yourself into poverty, Medicaid sets in, and then your physical condition improves and you no longer need nursing home care—then what?

Other Medicaid benefits vary from state to state, but Medicaid does pay some or all of Medicare premiums and may also pay for deductibles, coinsurance, and even outpatient prescription drugs for elderly with limited means and incomes below the poverty level or barely above it, ("limited means" being interpreted in 1999 as having "bank accounts, stocks, bonds or other resources not to exceed $4,000 for an individual or $6,000 for a couple"). Medicaid is certainly a step in the right direction toward universal health care; but once again, you have to be really poor or spend yourself into poverty before you are entitled to health care that you cannot afford on your own. And without federal controls, there is no assurance as to the benefits different states will want to or will be able to extend to the needy.

For almost 200 years, our government did little if anything to protect the health of the poor. This changed in 1965 when Medicaid put a safety net under the health care needs of America's disadvantaged. But now, we are told that we must put an end to such "entitlements," we must cut funding for them drastically, we may even have to dismantle altogether Washington's promise to our most vulnerable citizens. "There is no other way," so the conventional wisdom has it. But of course, there *is* another way. Is it not possible to imagine a society that taxes itself, and especially the upper-income earners, more heavily to provide satisfactory medical care for everyone, a society that rations health care not by wealth but by other criteria such as need? This may seem unthinkable in our current cut-taxes-cut-expenditures, antigovernment climate. But it is certainly a possible solution. After all, it has been adopted by virtually all industrialized countries.

Our government has taken steps in recent years, but although they are steps in the right direction, they are, unfortunately, totally inadequate, inadequate to give us the protection we need, inadequate as compared with other industrialized nations. Take the Family Leave Bill, for instance, finally passed after a prolonged struggle in Congress, that allows women to take an *unpaid* maternity leave without losing their jobs. Great: but what's a poor working mother going to do with an *unpaid* leave? She can't afford it. The EC (European Community) agreed, in November 1992, that all member states must give pregnant or breast feeding women a *minimum leave of 14 weeks at standard sick pay*, must allow them to switch from night to day shifts, exempt them from any work detrimental to their health, and let them take paid time off for prenatal checkups. All this, however, really applies only to England, Ireland, and Portugal because all the rest of Europe's member nations had already adopted higher standards (for instance France 16 weeks at 90 percent pay, Germany 14 to 19 weeks at 100 percent pay, or Sweden 38 weeks at 90 percent pay). Why can't we do the same for our working mothers? Or take the Kassebaum–Kennedy Health Care Portability Bill of 1996, a bill sponsored by one Republican and one Democratic senator, a bill with good intentions, a small step on a long road, but certainly not good enough either. This bill gives employees who lose their jobs or resign from them the right to take their insurance with them; in other words, it mandates insurers to renew policies even if the worker has developed a chronic illness. Most Americans will agree that that's good, that's the way it should be. However, this bill obviously does nothing for the 42 million uninsured nor for those unable to pay on their own for the previously employer-provided insurance; and it says nothing about premiums, which means that private insurance companies are allowed to raise them at will without any government-imposed limit.

To give just one more example, Congress, before adjourning in 1996, stopped "drive through deliveries," giving pregnant women with normal delivery the right under any insurance policy to stay two nights in the hospital, not just one—surely a significant improvement but far below the average hospital stay of new mothers in Europe.

Well-intentioned as they may be, such meager, bandage-type attempts don't begin to address our nation's health care problems; the measures proposed to preserve Medicare and Medicaid for future generations are likewise no more than temporary first-aid-type treatments; but joining all the other industrialized nations that have made health care a birthright of all their citizens is presently not even under consideration. We ought to know by now that we cannot turn to the free market for answers any more than we could call on it to provide us with stop signs, pollution-free rivers, or police protection. *We need to revamp our entire health care system.*

Unlikely as it may seem in today's special-interest-dominated political environment, the day will come when we will give careful consideration to a real cure, a system that replaces the over 1,500 private insurers with a single payer and allows you to go to the doctor of your choice. Such a system would provide cradle-to-grave health care coverage for all our inhabitants while assuring a decent income for our hardworking physicians and nurses, and it would eliminate the enormous waste of 1,500 competing private insurance companies when only one single payer is necessary.

Would such a single-payer system, adapted to American needs, solve all the problems in the area of health care? Obviously not. There remains the age-old economic problem of limited resources, insufficient to meet all needs, and the necessity of putting what is available to its best use. Most medical expenses occur in the last few months of a person's life, and because people are living longer, some really tough decisions will have to be made. Should scarce dialysis equipment be used to continue treatment of an 85-year-old man with terminal cancer? (England has limited public funding of dialysis treatment to patients under 65). Should public health care pay for a risky and very expensive double coronary bypass operation for a 91-year-old with multiple illnesses, whose life expectancy may perhaps be increased by six months or a year? Should organs for transplants be given to people infected with the AIDS virus? (Most American transplant centers say that the shortage of donated organs demands that they be reserved for those with the greatest chance of a long and productive life). It is these kinds of tough decisions that administrators of a single-payer health care system would be called on to make; but what such a system can and would provide is a guarantee of basic, fundamental health care for all, without the necessity of any individuals to spend themselves into poverty. (Of course, no matter what the health care system, in a capitalist society individuals can always use their private resources, if they so choose, for most kinds of treatment that public health care does not offer [though usually not for organ transplants].)

Those who advocate a single-payer system frequently give Canada as an example (although actually, the central government foots only one-third of the expenses there, the individual provinces the rest.) The system we may adapt at some future date will in all likelihood differ from the Canadian system in many ways. But in the meantime, powerful private health care interests and their supporters in the United States have spread such myths and untruths about it that the general public is fearful of "too much government" in health care.

Under such a government health insurance system, we are told, *you wouldn't be able to choose your own doctor*. WRONG. In Canada you can go to any doctor of your choice; if you are enrolled in an HMO in the United States you usually cannot. *"Socialized medicine—a cure worse than the disease,"* former President Bush called it. WRONG. Canada does not have a socialized medical system; Canadian physicians are not employees of the state. They are independent; they decide where they want to set up their practice, what hours they want to work, which patients they want to accept, which hospitals they want to associate with. They are private practitioners, working on an old-fashioned fee-for-service basis, albeit at fixed fees per patient visit or procedure, so that they have no incentive to prefer one patient over another. The major difference is that instead of sending their bills to hundreds of different clients and insurance companies, they send them all to just one place, the proper provincial government office. *"When you nationalize health care, you push costs higher, far higher,"* Bush said. WRONG. Quite apart from the fact that Canada's system is not really "nationalized" (as said before, doctors are not employees of the state), our health care costs are the highest in the world. Canada has three billing clerks for every 50 we have in the United States. There is no need for competitive advertising, lobbying, campaign contributions, enormous salaries for CEOs, huge profits for investors. It's no wonder that their administrative costs are less than half of ours (and so, by the way, are those of other countries with single-payer systems like Germany, France, the Netherlands, Australia, and Japan); and Canada's per person medical expenditure is 39 percent lower than it is in the United States and they cover everyone. Senator Paul Tsongas charged that *bone-marrow transplants (that he needed to treat his cancer) would not have been available in Canada* and he would have died. WRONG. Of course, Canada has bone-marrow transplants; actually, the pioneering work in that field was done by two Canadian physicians at the Ontario Cancer Institute—and Canada is well ahead of the United States in overall life expectancy and infant mortality rates. (Unfortunately, Senator Tsongas died of the disease in January 1997.) *"Canadians have no faith in their health care system; why would they otherwise come to the United States for their operations?"* WRONG. Study after study shows that the overwhelming majority of Canadians would not trade their health care system for ours (see, for instance, the *Journal of the American Medical Association*, October 23–30, 1990 or *The New Yorker*, April 20, 1992), while the United States always ranks last in public satisfaction. And, of course, the overwhelming majority of Canadians never come to the United States for treatment. Yes, we do have many more MRI systems and other advanced equipment, and so the very wealthiest Canadians do sometimes come here for certain procedures—it has to be the wealthiest because treatment here is very expensive and regular Canadian insurance would not cover it. Actually, the better part of Canadian medical spending in the United States reflects the migration of mostly elderly Canadians to Florida, Southern California, and other warmer spots during the winter, and their need for health care while there. *Canadians "have to wait in line for everything."* WRONG AGAIN, at least in part. Waits for regular appointments with family physicians are minimal. When it comes to surgery, that's a different matter. An appendectomy or a c-section? Have no fear, you'll be taken immediately. But if you want a wart removed because it doesn't look nice, you may have to wait quite a while or pay for it yourself (in addition to the national program, privately paid health care is always readily available, not only in Canada but in most "single-payer" system countries). However, it cannot be denied that the access to sophisticated technology is not as readily available as one wished it were. And, true, long waiting periods can be a problem. When a Canadian doctor calls a patient's coronary bypass surgery "elective" because he or she considers it necessary but not of immediate urgency, and therefore postpones it for several months—that can be frustrating. Such action, however, cannot be attributed to any investor's greed but simply to shortages of funds that often necessitate allocation of scarce resources according to medical urgency. "Faced with increasing costs," a Canadian doctor told this author in Quebec, "our provincial governments are under pressure to limit expenditures, trying for instance to have doctors replace labeled prescription medicines by cheaper generic drugs or using MRIs only when really necessary. So we Canadians grumble a bit," he said, "but we are aware that overall we have top notch medical care, and we certainly would not want to replace our health care system by any other." When we are critical of such shortcomings, let's be aware that in the United States, an uninsured family without money to pay for treatment doesn't have any doctor to go to. If their child gets an illness—whether an earache, the flu, or a more severe predicament—they are forced to take the youngster to the emergency room, where they often have to wait a long time and find it difficult to be referred to a specialist or for high-technology tests and treatments. And, if the uninsured need a root canal, eyeglasses, or a hearing aid, they simply can't get them at all without paying for them (unless of course, they are on Medicaid.) The Canadian approach, on the other hand, still stresses universal health coverage over all else. Nothing holds a more sacred place in the shrine of Canada's values than the country's health care system, and Canadians feel strongly that it reflects their regard for generosity and compassion. Neither they, nor for that matter any other industrialized country in the world, have shown any willingness to trade their health care system for ours; and when they learn that in the United States, at times of economic prosperity, 43 million are uninsured, and when they hear horror stories of families losing their life savings to pay for expensive medical procedures, they develop new patience for the flaws of their own system. *Canadian doctors are so underpaid, they all wish they could leave and practice here.* WRONG. They all could leave if they wanted to. There are plenty of job offerings in the United States published in Canadian medical journals and they'd have no difficulty getting permission to stay and practice here. Still, according to a Canadian source, only 1 percent of Canada's 55,000 physicians have chosen to do so. Yes, they'd make here one and a half, two times, or more what they are making in Canada. But there, they get low-cost education (including expenses to go back to school and become a specialist if they so choose); the nurses, receptionists, and equipment are paid for in hospital practices (as in Europe, hospital practices are separated from office practices); malpractice suits are few and far apart and frivolous malpractice suits are virtually unheard of, largely because Canadian lawyers don't work on a contingency basis but expect to be paid, win or lose; and Canadian doctors don't have to worry either about patients who are late with their payments or don't pay their bills at all. They just send their bills to the proper government office and receive their checks. It makes them feel good, some Canadian doctors told me, that they take care of all in need of their services without having to check on the patient's ability to pay their bills. (In other single-payer-system countries, likewise, physicians' incomes are respectable, albeit lower than in the United States. In Germany, for instance, gross income of family practitioners is over $100,000 per year, urologists earn at least 50 percent more, orthopedists about twice as much, two-thirds of it paid by the state, one-third by private patients).

It took us almost a century to assure at least a minimum of education to every American child, but we eventually did it. While the details of our future health care system will have to be worked out, it will hopefully also be based on the fundamental principle that health care, like education, should be every American's birthright. But it would seem difficult to achieve such a goal unless we were willing to convert our present system—our more than 1,500 health insurers, our Medicare, our Medicaid system—into some kind of a single-payer system that serves all. We are behind all other industrialized countries, more than half a century behind England. Perhaps Winston Churchill was right when he said, "The United States can be counted on doing the right thing after she has exhausted every other remedy."

Chapter 11

Education: We Can't Do Without It

In his 1997 State of the Union address, President Clinton made education the centerpiece of his speech and his top priority. He called for national education standards (tests to be paid for by the federal government and administered by individual states and school districts), for opening the doors of college education to everyone, and, at a time when cutting social programs was the vogue of the day, he asked for a substantial (20 percent) increase in government spending on education. Then, in 1999, he reiterated his request for additional federal funding of education. And true, in an era when technology advances with breathtaking speed, the paramount importance of education, both to the individual and to society, can hardly be overemphasized. Where do we stand?

In fact, close to half of our elderly can't read well enough to understand instructions on bottles telling them how to take their medicines; only around 85 percent of our adult population is functionally literate; only one-third of twelfth-graders can handle difficult reading material; in an international achievement test given to eighth-graders of 41 countries we ranked twenty-eighth in mathematics and seventeenth in science; and the average college junior with two years of college education completed would find it difficult to pass the *Abitur*, the test required of German teenagers to graduate from high school.

Inadequate teacher preparation, weak curricula, low-ebb student interest, "too much television," and other factors certainly contribute to our educational gap and merit thorough study. These issues, however, are beyond the scope of this book. Here we want to call attention to and address a major factor that permeates all aspects of our society: the difference in services offered to the well-to-do and to the poor and the resulting perpetuation of the cycle of poverty, both the result and the cause of much of our educational gap.

A thorough, solid education in the early years is the most appropriate way for a young child to get a good start in life; and more advanced education later on is the ticket for the children of low-income families to higher-paying levels. Full-time employees over 25 holding a college degree earn 50 percent more than those who merely graduate from high school, twice as much as those who don't finish high school. Holders of graduate degrees, on the average, earn 60 percent more than those with only a BS or BA degree.

Our modern economy imposes severe financial penalties on the inadequately skilled. But from preschool and kindergarten to higher education, the access to high-quality education is not equal; and the gap between the kind of education provided to children of wealthy and to children of poor families has been widening.

In the suburbs, you will find private schools for preschoolers, 12 to 15 in a room, with two well-trained, dedicated teachers able to give each child individual attention, with classrooms full of educational materials, toys, games, art supplies, and large, generously equipped playgrounds. Private suburban grade and high schools, alike, are located in clean, modern buildings, are fully equipped, including computers, and in general provide a wholesome environment. Compare this with most inner city schools, classes of 32 or more to a teacher, few books and other supplies, often dirty, old, worn-out furniture, broken windows, at times cockroach-infested kitchens without running water (as reported, for instance, in May 1996 by the New York Health Department).

In the clean, pleasant, fun-filled suburban environments, most children love to go to school; in the inner cities, the majority resent it. And it's not just private versus public schools; even public schools themselves differ greatly. Mostly financed from local property taxes, the ones in wealthy sections of town are generally clean, well funded, well staffed, and well supplied. American youths from poorer neighborhoods, disadvantaged by poverty and with parents unable to give them the background, the food, and the clothing that even middle-class children take for granted, are faced with unequal educational opportunities as well. No wonder our high school dropout rate is so high, 25 percent overall (much higher, of course, in the disadvantaged areas), the second highest after Mexico in the 29-member OECD (the Organization for Economic Cooperation and Development), as compared, for instance, with 9 percent in Germany and 6 percent in Japan. So it can hardly come as a surprise that, denied equal opportunity and with little hope for a brighter future, so many are much more likely to see course assignments as worthless, burdensome chores, to ignore teachers' instructions, to evidence disruptive behavior; to turn to drugs and violence; and even to embark early on a life of crime.

There can't be real equality, real educational progress unless we see to it that all public schools are equally well equipped and staffed. It's a problem, to be sure, to attract good teachers to inner city school jobs, certainly the least desirable in the profession. With insufficient funds for schooling in these areas, government subsidies will be necessary to underwrite higher teacher salaries; or alternately, as proposed by Creative Policy Solutions of Kensington, California, a 100 percent federal income tax exclusion could be applied to all teachers' salaries earned in federally designated poverty areas as an incentive for good teachers with seniority to accept positions there. (President Clinton recently took a step in this direction. In his 1999 budget proposal he asked for substantial increases in college funds for students willing to teach in inner-city schools and on Indian reservations.)

And higher education? In many foreign countries, such as Germany, Greece, or England, a college education is still free for those who qualify scholastically; in others such as Australia or Holland, it's relatively inexpensive, around $1,200 a year. In the United States, on the other hand, tuition is high, averaging over $3,000 a year in four-year public institutions and over $13,500 in private colleges and universities (up to $7,000 and more in some of the former and over $20,000 at places such as Harvard, Yale, or Stanford). Add to this room and board and expenditures for books and supplies, and it is clear that without subsidization, a college education would be well-nigh impossible to attain for the sons and daughters of low-income households and may present financial problems to middle-class families also.

But, to be sure, need-based assistance is available to college students with inadequate financial means. Federally underwritten Pell grants, supplemented by Federal Supplemental Educational Opportunity grants, President Clinton's Americorps program that offers education vouchers in exchange for a year of minimum-income volunteer work, federally subsidized work-study programs that provide part-time, on-campus, usually minimum-wage jobs, a $1,500 tax credit for parents of college students (obviously not of much use to the most needy who pay no or little taxes)—all are of help in overcoming financial difficulties. And there are federal student loan programs, used by millions of college and university students. Moreover, most state colleges and universities offer additional need-based financial assistance.

All of these programs are limited in amounts available to applicants, and student loans can be burdensome during years of payback periods; but the fact remains that need-based financial aid is available. Why is it, then, that so relatively few of the financially disadvantaged young men and women take advantage of opportunities offered? Why is it that among children of the poorest one-fifth of our population, only one in 20 ever goes to a four-year college (among the poorest 5 or 10 percent, the percentage is much lower still), while three out of every four children of the top 20 percent of income earners get a college or university education?

Mostly from homes where parents lack a good education and where exposure to books and to intellectual stimulation in the early years is not the norm, coming from second-rate grade and high schools which often makes it difficult to compete for admission to better colleges and universities, and ill-prepared to meet the challenges of higher education, teenagers from low-income families often lack the motivation even to think of college and a professional career. Certainly, families and the community may have to play a major role in stimulating and encouraging youngsters and in kindling in them the desire to learn and "to make something of themselves" (and a difficult task this often is); but if we want to help prepare *all* our children for the educational challenges of modern times, it becomes the moral and the economic obligation of government to provide the funding necessary to bring quality education to disadvantaged areas bereft of adequate educational facilities, supplies, and teachers. And, to be sure, our government has taken steps, however inadequate as they may still be, to correct the injustices of the past. Admittedly, it's difficult in these cut-government-expenditures, balance-the-budget days, but we cannot make our educational goals come true unless we keep and expand the programs we have, and develop new ones aimed at some day making equality of educational opportunities a reality throughout our land.

Since the mid-1960s, the Headstart program has served primarily four-year-olds from disadvantaged families, providing them with comprehensive health, education, and social services prior to entering school. It is an excellent example of how government can enhance the opportunities of low-income families and their children. It gives these youngsters the opportunity to enter school on a more equal footing with others, and the results speak for themselves. As compared with children from similar backgrounds who have not taken part in this or similar educational programs, these preschoolers are twice as likely to be literate, to go to college, or to get a job. They are less likely to have a run-in with the law, and they are only half as likely to have a teenage pregnancy or to get on welfare. For every dollar spent on Headstart, we save six dollars on welfare, social services, crime, and other expenditures. Unfortunately, there is no room in Headstart centers for even half of all qualifying children who could benefit from the program. To increase funding for Headstart clearly makes sense from a moral as well as an economic perspective; to trim such increases would seem ill-advised and counterproductive. Still, when in 1997, President Clinton asked for a $700 million increase, Congress reduced it to $200 million. To cut Headstart appropriations or to abolish the program altogether, as some have proposed, would not only be unconscionable, but also irrational from an economic point of view.

Apart from attempts to reduce or eliminate funding for student loans and for Headstart, other proposals have been offered in the past few years that would greatly harm plans to improve education in the United States. Among these are proposals to eliminate the subsidy that finances waivers of interest on student loans until the student leaves college and joins the workforce; to dismantle Americorps; to abolish the Department of Education; to prevent illegal immigrant children and teenagers whose papers are under revision from attending public schools, virtually sending them out into the streets to participate in gang activities; and to offer parents who send their children to religious or other private schools vouchers to help them pay for it.

The voucher proposal made during the 1995 presidential campaign would offer parents a choice: send your children to public schools or, alternately, the government will send you a voucher for $1,500 per year per child, enabling them to go to the school of their choice, "just as does the child of the President of the United States," so the argument went. Unfortunately, private schools cost much, much more than $1,500 a year. The assistance may be of help to some middle-class families who can afford to come up with the rest themselves, but a poor family with two or three children would hardly be able to shell out the extra money to pay for a reasonably priced $6,000-a-year private school. On the other hand, wealthy families who send their children to private schools anyhow would get a $1,500 per child bonanza. The billions of dollars needed to support such a program would surely not come from increased allocations for education. They would come from a reduction of funds available for public education. One can't help but wonder whether advocates of the voucher system actually want to help low-income families to go to private schools or whether their real goal is siphoning money away from public schools already facing enormous financial burdens and destroy public education in the United States.

Although not an integral part of the American school system as such, a chapter on education would not be complete without a word about the much-embattled NEA, the National Endowment for the Arts. Over the years, the NEA has used its funds to provide matching grants for high school theater groups and to help finance museum exhibitions, community theaters, public radio and television arts broadcasts, orchestra and chamber music concerts, and other worthwhile art projects. Its opponents attack it on two grounds, economic (the arts should be financed by private individuals and organizations, not the government), and moral (why should we subsidize obscene and blasphemous art?) Both arguments are untenable. Private individuals and organizations do contribute to the arts, but with so many worthwhile charities in need of money they can't raise enough to fill the gap. And the government commitment to the arts can hardly be called extravagant: the amount allocated to the NEA in 1996 was under $100 million, not enough to keep the Pentagon going for three and a half hours. As to moral objections: Art is in the eyes of the beholder; still, some very few grants may have been objectionable and should perhaps not have been funded. But if we find a U.S. Senator to be unworthy of his position, we don't abolish the Senate, do we? Over 110,000 grants have been funded by the NEA since 1965, and complaints were raised against only 30 of them, one in over 3,000. Still, in July 1997, the House, by a one-vote majority, managed to deny the NEA a penny, but the Senate voted to fund it again. So, in the end, it survived and in the 1998 budget the allocation was cut by only one million, to $98 million. Regrettably, this is no guarantee that the NEA will survive in the long run.

Who would be willing to estimate the value of just one more Einstein, just one more Edison? Can we really afford to curtail expenditures for our schools? No, we cannot. Every dollar spent on education pays off handsomely in the future. Looking at it from the other side, it costs an average of $6,100 a year to keep a student in school, $30,000 to keep a criminal in prison—more than to send him to Harvard for a year. If a corporation could be sure to get the services of a college graduate for life, it would not hesitate to "invest" in higher education. Since this is not the case, education logically gets short shrift from the private sector. But the nation as a whole does get the services of well-prepared citizens for all their lives.

In this day and age, an educated populace is more necessary than ever. Undoubtedly, families, teachers, schools, and local schoolboards all share in the responsibility of promoting education in our country. But to achieve the goals envisioned for the twenty-first century—in our interest, in the interest of our children and of generations yet to come, and regardless of budget-balancing considerations—a firm government commitment to education, financed by our tax dollars, is definitely called for. As Lyndon B. Johnson said some 36 years ago, in 1963, "once we considered education a public expense, now we know it is a public investment."

Chapter 12

The Environment: More Economic Growth or a More Livable Planet? A Delicate Balance

Pollution of air and water, depletion of the soil, rapid shrinkage of the land area available for agriculture, gradual disappearance of forests and wetlands, and extermination of ever more species of wildlife—all are accompaniments of modern-day economic evolution, not only in the industrial world but to a somewhat lesser extent in developing countries as well. And in all these respects, the United States does more damage to the environment than any other country. With less than 5 percent of the world's population and 7 percent of the world's land mass, we are number one in the world in hazardous waste, in contribution to acid rain, in major oil spills affecting coastal areas, in per capita number of cars, gasoline consumption, emission of air pollutants, output of garbage. Our carbon emission is twice as high per person than that of Japan or Russia, 14 times as high as that of Brazil—it is almost one-fourth of the world's total. Suburban sprawl, in the United States, keeps converting pastures, cornfields, and forest lands into subdivisions at the rate of one million acres a year; and 45,000 deaths a year are attributed to air pollution alone.

One can hardly question the benefits of economic development that have catapulted countless millions into higher standards of living throughout the developed countries (although the distribution of the wealth, so created, leaves much to be desired everywhere). But economic growth does not come free, and the first and perhaps foremost price to be paid is the encroachment on the natural environment.

The confrontation between further economic growth and environmental costs, between more production and ecological decay, merits serious examination. The more advanced, industrialized countries may have reached a level at which the cost of additional growth is too high; there, in other words, the loss of environmental quality exceeds the benefits. But this does not apply equally to all kinds of economic growth, and the advanced countries need to consider the kind of growth they can afford. After all, increasing services such as those provided by teachers, social workers, and performers does much less damage to the environment than increasing the production of automobiles, fur coats, or plastic bags. The continuous replacement and gradual improvements of existing consumer and capital goods (goods needed to produce other goods such as tools and machinery) must of course continue, but the protection of the environment calls for careful regulation of allowable pollutant levels, disposal of waste, and what have you. We do need paper, but we don't want to devastate our historic forests; we do need factories, but we do not want to poison the environment. We have to strike a delicate balance between our needs for goods and services and the kind of world we want to leave behind for future generations.

Under our profit-driven value system, we measure the value of a tree by its pulp and by the two-by-fours we can make from it, refusing to acknowledge its value for the environment—how it protects the soil, produces oxygen, and adds shade and beauty to our countryside. Do we really want our children to inherit an environment of cities with hard-to-breathe, dirty air, water unsafe to drink, countrysides of tree stumps where once stood magnificent forests, birds disappearing, salmon and trout gone forever? The question is not what it costs if we become a more environment-conscious society; the question is what it'll cost if we don't.

Some 30 years ago, by the end of the 1960s, California mothers evidenced concentrations of DDT so high that their milk would have been barred from interstate commerce had it been in any other container; and in England, they couldn't legally have eaten any Americans since their bodies contained more DDT than the permissible limit under British law. Since 1970, however, major laws have been passed in the United States to clean up the air and the water in our rivers and lakes, to provide good, potable drinking water, to protect endangered species, and to make sure that landfills are safely operated. These laws certainly had a positive effect on the health of our inhabitants; but by the 1990s we had become aware that they were not enough and that more stringent legislation and stricter enforcement were a necessity. The Food Quality Protection Act of 1996 became the cornerstone of new legislative efforts to ensure the quality of our nation's food and water. It formalized safety standards that would require "a reasonable certainty of no harm" for all foods treated with pesticides (for instance, no more than one in a million chance of getting cancer from lifetime exposure) and ordered the EPA (Environmental Protection Agency) to test the safety of about 9,000 agricultural chemicals, with emphasis on their effect on children, who are more susceptible. Other environmental laws and ordinances followed in quick succession such as the 1996 Safe Drinking Water Act and President Clinton's directive to overhaul the country's system of meat and poultry inspection. California went even further than the federal government. In 1997, it became the first state to regulate *consumer* products that pollute the air. By order of the state's air board, more than 3,000 consumer products including automotive polishes, dishwasher detergents, herbicides, insecticides, lubricants, carpet cleaners, and hair sprays must meet new pollution limits that will cut their smog-causing fumes and other harmful effects in half. Manufacturers obviously fear that reformulation of their products will be costly and make them less effective, and that the manufacture of some products may have to be discontinued altogether. But the air board's decision was unanimous and is not likely to be abrogated.

Still, the battle is far from over; as a matter of fact, it has just started. Under the influence of special interests from the timber, oil, mining, and other industries, anti-environmentalists in Congress would, for instance, want to reverse the environmental laws that protect the Alaskan arctic wildlife refuge and open the area to exploitation by oil and gas companies. They'd like to start the process of selling off national parks, relax restrictions on cancer-causing substances in food, ease control over industrial pollutants, restrict protection of the wetlands, and gut the Endangered Species Act by killing the funds for its enforcement. Our children could still see the Florida panther—on a video or in a museum, of course. The proposed and misnamed Job Creation and Wage Enforcement Act is an example of their tactics and goals. Under this law, the government would compensate property owners for reducing the value of their business or property resulting from federal regulations. Land and property values had increased in the first place because the government built or subsidized nearby roads, freeways, bridges, water and sewer connections, or nearby airports; but any regulation designed to protect the public from harmful usage of private property would call for compensation of the owners to the extent that it reduces the value of their property!

Sometimes laws are enacted without sufficient cost-benefit (environmental-cost-versus-current-production-benefit) analysis. An example is the Salvage Timber Rider President Clinton signed in 1996. It enables lumber companies to denude forests and wetlands of beautiful trees. Clinton has since admitted that he should never have put his signature onto this law and promised to work for its repeal—an effort not likely to meet with success in the near future.

Recently, anti-environmentalists on Capital Hill, who had long tried to weaken the EPA, have moderated their rhetoric and abandoned much of their agenda because public opinion polls showed that most Americans and particularly women and suburban voters did not share their views. In October 1995, a survey by the Council for Excellence in Government found that nearly 90 percent of respondents considered it necessary for the government to make sure that American businesses do not unduly harm the environment and 70 percent felt that government action was necessary to ensure safe products and working conditions. But, unfortunately, at election time, people's actions are not always reflective of their own beliefs. As voters they frequently assume that the government will adequately protect their air, water, and environment and so, at the voting booth, they often do not give enough consideration to the candidates' stands on these issues; and as consumers they tend to pay little attention to the environmental consequences of products they use. To illustrate, when in the mid-1980s inhabitants of much-polluted Los Angeles were asked whether it needed a new rapid transportation system to cut down on its largely automobile-caused air pollution, 86.6 percent said "yes." But when they were subsequently asked, "if by some miracle a rapid transportation system were in effect tomorrow, would you ride on it," 50 percent said "no" and only 4.7 percent said they definitely would. In other words, they wanted others to use it to reduce the smog, but they did not want to inconvenience themselves.

The water, air, and soil are here for all of us to share; our forefathers left them to us, and it's the inheritance we leave our children. When we cut Medicaid or welfare and realize that we did wrong, we can correct the mistakes, albeit not always for those already detrimentally affected. However, failure to protect the environment can cause long-lasting and often permanent damage, and the destruction of endangered species is irreversible.

But the question arises: Why would producers want to pollute the air and the water that they and their children breathe and drink, or harm nature in other ways? Would not common sense dictate that they themselves, out of their own free will, protect the environment in which they live? Do we really need the government to legislate and regulate? Can't we leave it up to the private sector, the free market, to act responsibly?

Unfortunately, we cannot. To survive under the pressure of competition, producers are often forced to engage in activities that are harmful to society—a problem known in economic parlance as "social costs versus private gains." Manufacturers as a whole are surely as good and as decent human beings as the rest of us. They don't want to pollute the air or the water any more than you and I. But they can't help it. For manufacturers to install equipment and introduce processes that would reduce the harm imposed on the environment by their activities is expensive. If they did, their cost of production would rise and they would find themselves at an economic disadvantage as compared with other firms in the field who didn't. Farmers whose crop yield would drop if they refrained from using fertilizer that raises the toxicity of the soil find themselves in a similar situation. But if we were to put a tax on polluters high enough so that it would be less expensive to remedy the problem than to pay the tax—now that would be a different matter, wouldn't it? So, once again, we have a problem that the free market, by its very nature, cannot solve on its own. The protection of the environment calls out for federal regulations and for their strict enforcement.

Chapter 13

Taxes: The Price We Pay for Living in a Civilized Society

In every society, no matter what the economic system, there are some goods and services that are not for sale. We enjoy them jointly, all of us together, and if you or I use them, we do not deprive others from using them also. In this sense, stop lights, police departments, or expenditures for the protection of the environment are different from hamburgers, automobiles, or hair cuts. So, together we contribute for such "public" goods and services. And as a society that wants to establish a safe and secure haven for all its citizens, we also contribute to other joint expenditures such as aid to a part of the country hard-hit by devastating storms, school lunches for children who otherwise wouldn't have enough to eat, or assistance to the poor among us who are unable to take care of themselves and their families on their own.

The financial contributions we make to maintain a civilized society are not voluntary; we impose them by law, for if we didn't, some among us might use our streets, our bridges, our parks and get all the benefits of government expenditures without paying their fair share. But the question is: what is a "fair share"?

Obviously, we cannot ask the poor to contribute as much as the rich. We cannot even ask them to pay the same percentage in taxes as the well-to-do. That's why a "fair" tax structure is so often interpreted as one which at least to some degree is progressive.

A "progressive" tax is one that takes not only more money but a larger proportion—a higher percentage—out of the income of the wealthier. But is that fair? How can we justify not merely higher taxes but even a higher tax rate for those with higher incomes? Indeed we can, from an economic as well as a moral point of view. There is what economists call *the law of diminishing marginal utility* (like other scientists, economists like to use difficult words for easily understandable concepts). That law says that the more you have of any given commodity at any one time, the less additional units mean to you. Take shoes, for instance. If you didn't have any, what wouldn't you be willing to give up, what sacrifices wouldn't you be willing to make to own a pair? A second pair is surely nice to have, but it is not of equal importance. And, if you had 25 pairs, you might not want a 26th, even if it were free. It would just be in your way. By the same token, a car, an overcoat, or even an ice cream cone, would mean so much more to you if you didn't have any, than a fifth one if you already had four. Well, that law also applies to money: one additional dollar obviously means less to someone who has many than to someone who has few. After all, when you tax really low-income earners, you tax away their necessities of life—the fruit or meat for their table, the oil that heats their homes on cold winter evenings; when you tax middle-income earners you may not tax away their necessities but you surely deprive them of some of their conveniences and pleasures— the camping van they had wanted for so long, the vacation in Europe they had been dreaming about for years; when you tax higher-income earners (say with annual income over $200,000), they can still afford their necessities, conveniences, and pleasures; you tax away only some of their luxuries—perhaps the new Mercedes or yacht. But, tax the wealthy, especially those with incomes in the millions, and you touch neither their necessities nor their conveniences nor even their luxuries. They can still afford them all. What you tax away is merely some of their savings and potential investments. Let's face it: those with an income of $2 million a year, subject to, let's say, a 50 percent tax rate, will surely manage on their million without too much deprivation; those with an annual income of $50,000 would suffer great hardships if they had to pay half of it in income taxes, and the family getting along on $25,000 would be driven below the poverty level by such a tax. Moreover, were it not for our income and estate taxes—the only somewhat progressive taxes we have—the gap between our rich and poor (discussed in greater detail in Chapter 5) would become even more unconscionable than it already is. We have 170 billionaires and multi-billionaires in our country (at 6 percent interest, even one billion would yield you returns of *over one hundred and fifty thousand dollars a day*), and we have many more whose holdings are over $100 million. Without progressive taxation, their accumulated wealth would soon reach yet more astronomical proportions. So let's take a look at the various taxes we have and evaluate the impact they have on different groups in our society.

The imposition of *federal income taxes* in the United States started in 1861, as a measure to help finance the Civil War, with a 3 percent tax on incomes between $600 and $10,000 a year (one dollar then bought what thirty buy today), and 5 percent thereafter. Abolished in the early 1870s, a subsequent Populist proposal of a 2 percent tax for incomes over $4,000 and 5 percent for the wealthiest brought charges of "confiscation" and "socialism," and predictions that it would dampen incentives. To avoid any future disputes as to the government's right to levy income taxes, the Sixteenth Amendment to the Constitution was passed in 1913, bestowing upon Congress the "power to lay and collect taxes on incomes, from whatever source derived" and made income tax the largest source of revenues for the federal government. It was particularly during the times of war and depression that we saw the need to tax the wealthiest among us at high rates. Under the 1918 World War Revenue Act, marginal taxes (taxes on earnings above a certain amount) were raised to 77 percent, for high-income earners, lowered thereafter, then raised again in 1935 to a maximum of 75 percent, and eventually to an all-time high of 93 percent on the wealthiest (family incomes of over $400,000 a year, $200,000 for single individuals) during World War II. Looking at it from this vantage point, our current marginal tax of 39.6 percent for incomes over $278,450 (single or family, in 1998) does not seem unreasonably high, and charges that if we'd raised it any higher we'd kill all incentives to work and produce for our "leading" citizens . . . well, we know better. When during World War II and in the immediate postwar era federal marginal income tax rates exceeded 90 percent for high-income earners, Bob Hope still told his jokes on the stage, investors still bought General Motors stock, and the neighborhood dentist didn't cut his working hours either. No indeed, the idea that millionaires will refuse to work or invest if we raise their income tax rate above the current 39.6 percent level is ludicrous. To deprive major parts of our population of much-needed government services to keep these taxes low or even reduce them further is unconscionable.

Most states also levy *state income taxes* (some states such as Florida, Nevada, or Texas do not). Although their maximum rates are relatively low, they are all progressive.

Corporations pay a *corporate income tax* with rates for 1998 varying from 15 percent for low-earning corporations (under $50,000), rising up to 39 percent for marginal (additional) earnings over $100,000 and below $335,000, inexplicably dropping thereafter to 34 percent for marginal incomes over $335,000 and below $10,000,000 (corporations this size must have better lobbyists in Washington), then rising again, and with a flat rate of 35 percent for *total* incomes over $18,000,000.

Corporations often retain part of their earnings for reserves and future expenditures. Then, on the part distributed in the form of dividends, the stockholders—the owners—have to pay their personal federal and state income taxes, a form of "double taxation," as it is often called. There is a reason, though, why corporations pay a special tax not levied on unincorporated single proprietorships or partnerships. As distinguished from these latter, a corporation has a life of its own, apart from the lives of its stockholders. It is, as Chief Justice John Marshall (1755–1835) explained over 150 years ago, "an artificial being, invisible, intangible, and existing only in the contemplation of the law," a definition that holds as true today as it did then. If all the stockholders of a corporation were to die on the same day, the corporation would continue; the ownership shares would just be passed on to the heirs. A corporation can be taken to court, and while you can't jail it, if can be fined or, in extreme cases, be sentenced to death, its existence extinguished. The reason why a corporation is granted by law the status of having a life of its own is so that the owners will not bear personal responsibility for anything that goes wrong. If you are in business for yourself and your enterprise fails, you might lose everything you have. But if you are a part owner of a corporation—you hold shares of common stock in it—the worst that can happen is that the corporation goes bankrupt and the value of your stock drops to zero. Bad enough, true, but you bear no financial responsibility for any remaining debts. It is largely because of this "limited liability," as it is called, that people incorporate their businesses and that so many are willing to buy shares of stock in large corporations, even if they know little or nothing about the business the corporations are engaged in, simply in the hope that their investment will yield decent returns. It is this separate life that a corporation enjoys, this limit on the financial responsibility of its shareholders, that gives our government—gives us—every right to tax it. And it also imposes on our government the obligation to protect shareholders from shady practices, to impose rules and regulations within which corporations must operate, and to see that they are enforced. Unfortunately (whether such regulations deal with labor contracts, protection of the environment, enforcing competition or whatever), officers, representatives and spokesmen of powerful multi-billion-dollar corporations have all too often been able to find loopholes, escape restrictive legislation, change the laws, or bend them to their interests—a fact so well-known that it hardly needs mentioning. And as to the importance of corporate income taxes to government revenues: in total, they account for 10 percent of taxes collected by the federal government, and for less than 2 percent levied by state and local governments.

To rein in somewhat the otherwise boundless accumulation of wealth by the few, *estate (inheritance) taxes* are an economic necessity for a civilized society. Without them, a $100-million untaxed inheritance would, at an annual after-income-tax rate of interest or profits of 5 percent, double within 14 years, quadruple in 28, increase eight-fold in 42, sixteen-fold in 56, and thirty-twofold to $3.2 billion in 70 years. Within another 70 years, at the same rate, the next generation of heirs would have increased their holdings to over $100 billion, and the next generation thereafter to over $3 trillion—actually, somewhat less, to be sure, since they'll spend some of their inheritance each year, but still an untenable situation.

Until 1997, the first $600,000 were free of federal estate taxes, and that was enough to protect the estates of most middle-income families (of the 40,000 individuals who pay estate taxes each year, 92 per cent come from the upper one-fifth, 81 percent from the upper one-twentieth, of income earners.) In early 1995, President Clinton proposed lowering the exemption and levying some taxes on estates over $200,000. Not only did his proposal fall on deaf ears, but the 1997 budget accord actually provides for a gradual increase in the exclusion, up to 625,000 by 1999, and scheduled to reach $1 million by 2006. This obviously does nothing for poor and lower middle-class families whose estates never come close even to $600,000. We can expect more public support for another provision that more than doubled the estate exemption for family-owned businesses and farms to $1.3 million, as of 1998. There is widespread feeling that heirs of family businesses and farms whose taxable values have gone up due to inflation and higher real estate prices should not be forced to sell them or take out huge loans to meet estate taxes. However, only 12 percent of all estate taxes collected come from such family businesses or farms; and to require millionaires to dispose of some of their stock and bond holdings to meet their inheritance tax obligations does not seem an unreasonable request. In any case, estate taxes are of relatively little significance, as far as government revenues are concerned: they amount to barely 1 percent of taxes collected by the federal government; and while they vary from state to state, they play but a very minor role in state tax collections also.

State and local governments collect about half as much in taxes as does the federal government. Roughly two-thirds of the $700 billion they take in annually comes from sales and property taxes, apportioned about equally between the two. The federal government does not levy general sales taxes; it does levy *excise taxes*, a kind of sales tax on specific items such as gasoline or tobacco.

Since everyone pays the same tax on goods and services purchased, you might get the impression that *sales taxes* are proportionate; they are not. They are highly *regressive*. Remember, a tax is progressive if it takes a larger *percentage* out of the *income* of the wealthier. Well, sales taxes rest more heavily on low-income earners. How come? Simply because the poorer have to spend more of their income on goods and services that carry a sales tax while the wealthier buy stock and bonds, take trips to Europe, put a part of their earnings into savings accounts, and thus pay sales tax on a much smaller percentage of their income. Some states such as California exempt food bought in grocery stores (though not necessarily food and drinks bought in restaurants), a tax structure obviously somewhat less regressive in nature since the poor spend a much larger part of their incomes on food than the upper-income earners.

State and local governments like sales taxes, in part because they are collected daily and hence provide a steady flow of money into state coffers. But there is another, perhaps more important reason: they are less objectionable to the general public. "The art of taxation," said Jean Baptiste Colbert, Finance Minister to Louis XIV, "consists of so plucking the goose as to obtain the largest amount of feathers with the least amount of hissing." Well, there isn't much hissing about sales taxes. It seems so little, just a few cents added per dollar spent; but does it ever add up, in total to the tune of well over a quarter of a *trillion* dollars per year! Try to raise income taxes or make them more progressive and you'll hear the hissing of the most powerful ganders from state capitals to Washington.

Property taxes tend to be more proportionate: If you have a $500,000 house and drive a $48,000 Mercedes while I live in a $125,000 house and drive a $12,000 Toyota, you pay four times as much in property taxes as I do, and the assumption is that you probably earn about four times as much. It's an assumption, to be sure, often far off, but this tax is still likely to be more proportionate than income or sales taxes. Yet, property taxes can, and often do, cause financial difficulties for the less well endowed. Take the 82-year-old widow, for example, who barely manages on her monthly social security check in her little one-family house that she and her husband paid off 20 years ago. Now, at times of rising real estate prices, the value of her house goes up and so do her property taxes. She isn't selling, because to rent a place would cost her much more; her fixed income (pensions, interest on bonds, etc.) may not change at all; the slight annual increase in social security disbursements is just enough to have them keep up with inflation; and her out-of-pocket medical expenses are likely to rise as she gets older; so she might find it quite difficult to cope with the rising property tax on her home.

In this era of reductions of social services for the needy and of lower taxes for those who don't need it, the proposal to cut in half or eliminate completely the *capital gains tax* is surely one of the most deceptive of propositions. Presented as a benefit to small businesses and farmers, it is nothing of the kind. This little understood tax is levied on profits derived from buying something, such as a painting or a piece of jewelry, and later selling it at a higher price than you paid for it. This tax does not apply to businesses selling their merchandise at a profit. On that they'll pay an income, not a capital gains tax. Obviously, small entrepreneurs will not benefit from any lowering of this tax unless they start a business or buy a farm with the intention of selling out again two or three years later at a profit. The lion's share of capital gains comes from the purchase and subsequent sale of corporate stocks. No wonder, then, that the top 1 percent of income earners account for almost one-half, and the top 20 percent for 90 or perhaps 98 percent of all capital gains (depending on which study you trust, the Congressional Committee's on Taxation or *Business Week's*).

If you are in a low-income tax bracket, you'd pay your low tax rate on any income, from whatever source derived. On the other hand, the *maximum* anyone would have had to pay in capital gains taxes, from 1987 to 1997, was 28 percent, well below the tax levied on the wealthy for income from other sources; but under the 1997 budget accord it was lowered to 20 percent (for assets held at least 18 months before sale.) So, on a $2,000 wage raise, the working man making $35,000 a year has to pay 28 percent in federal income taxes while the multi-millionaire making $200,000 on the sale of stock pays only 20 percent—or eventually nothing at all if the opponents of the capital gains tax who want to abolish it altogether ever get their way. (A special provision lowering the capital gains tax to 10 percent for couples earning less than $41,200 in 1998 is but a meaningless breadcrumb thrown to low-income earners, since they are very unlikely ever to have any capital gains to report. It's like telling a couple barely above the poverty line that they can get a discount whenever they buy a $6-million house in Laguna Beach.) The argument that well-heeled Americans who are the main beneficiaries of this tax deduction would invest their savings into new factories, new machinery, or other productive activities that would benefit the rest of us is the same ludicrous supply-side economics, feed-the-horse-so-that-the-sparrows-may-eat theory discussed earlier. Why should other, lower income earners have to pay more taxes so that the investment activities of the wealthier can be taxed at a lower rate? In any case, there is no reason to assume that these latter would not spend the extra money on French champagne, Japanese cars, or trips to fancy resorts in Latin America. Clinton's secretary of the treasury, Robert Rubin, who used to be on the board of the New York Stock Exchange and had seen enough fortunes made on Wall Street to know that speculators don't need a tax break to jump start their investments, felt that reducing the capital gains tax was "a bad idea;" but reduced it was. Surely President Clinton's proposal to eliminate capital gains taxes on homes but not on other assets such as stocks or rare paintings would seem to make much more sense. And indeed, the 1997 budget accord provided for it: a couple does not have to report the sale of their home on their tax return as long as the selling price is under $500,000 ($250,000 for a single individual).

With tax cutting so high on the political agenda, one would think that its loudest proponents would also favor reducing the taxes of low-income workers. Not so, I am afraid. They took Clinton to task for having introduced in his first two years in office what they called "the largest tax increase" in our country's history. Technically, in number of dollars, they may be right. But the fact is that in 1993 he and his then Democratic Congress raised taxes only on the highest 1.2 percent of income earners and the upper 13 percent of social security recipients. For the next 82 percent of families the tax remained the same. And for the lowest 16 percent of income earners, taxes were actually reduced. This last feat was accomplished by simply raising the earned income credit.

The *earned income credit* was started under the Ford administration. Hailed as "the best way of welfare," by Ronald Reagan, it gives low-income working people a tax refund on their "earned income" (income from wages) of up to $341 in 1999 for an individual or couple, and up to $3,756 for an individual or family with more than one child—a refund given, by the way, even if no taxes are owed. This tax credit currently affects 15 million working families. The 1994 increase in the earned income credit actually pulled two million working families out of poverty, instead of taxing them into poverty, and it surely provides a strong incentive for the poor to get off welfare and go to work. To reduce or eliminate the earned income credit altogether would be nothing less than an almost unbearable tax increase on the working poor. But unbelievable as it may seem, in the late 1990s many of the same legislators who champion raising the estate tax exemption and lowering or eliminating capital gains taxes are advocating just that.

A *tax credit*, say of $1,000, (be it for child care, for taxes paid to foreign countries, or what have you) is subtracted directly from the taxes you owe and thus allows you and everyone else entitled to it—whether rich, middle-class, or poor—the same $1,000 tax reduction; but it still does nothing for those who don't earn enough to pay income taxes and little for those whose taxes are less than the $1,000 credit they are entitled to (except in rare cases such as the earned income credit, where the tax credit is "negative" also, meaning that if the taxpayer owes less in taxes than the credit he is entitled to, the difference will be paid to him by the government). A tax deduction on the other hand (such as interest on your mortgage payment) is weighted heavily in favor of high-income earners. Since deductions allow you to take the amounts to be deducted off your income before figuring your "taxable income," they once again obviously do nothing for the individual who doesn't earn enough to pay taxes. As to those who do pay taxes, if they are low-income earners in the 15 percent tax bracket, a $1,000 tax deduction will save them $150; but if their earnings are $200,000 a year and they are in the 36 percent bracket, the same $1,000 deduction will reduce their taxes by $360.

While other taxes such as social security and Medicare taxes have been discussed elsewhere, this chapter should not be ended without reference to the *flat tax.* In vogue during the 1995 presidential campaign as a proposal to revamp our entire tax system, this dream of the rich, embraced also by some middle-class and low-income earners, is likely to raise its head again at some future time. The basic idea is that after a certain deduction—somewhere between $20,000 to $30,000 per family—everyone would pay taxes at the same rate (usually proposed at between 15 and 19 percent) on incomes beyond that.

Over the years, Congress tried to overhaul our tax code 11 times with the intention of simplifying it, and each attempt has made it more complex. Today, Americans spend some 400 million hours a year preparing their income taxes, and an estimated 10 percent of all returns contain mathematical errors. The main appeal of the flat tax is that it would make filling out your tax return a simple five-minute procedure. But, beyond that, it has little merit. It reminds one of American writer, editor, and social critic H.L. Mencken's statement that "for every problem there is a solution which is simple, neat—and wrong."

Flat tax advocates propose a system under which a $5,000 wage increase for the middle-class income earners would be taxed at the same rate as a $5,000 increase in profits by the multi-millionaire. Our tax is flat enough as it is—too flat, as a matter of fact, some would say. To carry it to such an extreme is ludicrous. No other industrialized country—to the knowledge of this author, no country anywhere—is even considering such an idea. But Malcolm "Steve" Forbes, Jr., self-financed presidential candidate and champion of the flat tax movement in the 1995 presidential campaign, whose wealth is estimated at somewhere between $90 and $400 million went even further: his flat tax proposal exempted capital gains and interest from taxation. So, under his proposal, if you worked hard and earned $50,000 a year, you'd get a $30,000 exemption and pay 17 percent, or $3,400, in taxes on the rest. He, on the other hand, may make millions in capital gains on the stock market and in interest on his bonds and he'd pay no tax at all. He didn't become president; he didn't even win his party's nomination. However, all too many influential individuals still think it's a good idea, but are sensible enough to realize that at least at present, the great majority of American voters wouldn't go for it, once they understood what it entailed.

Relatively low as income taxes of upper-income earners are, they can even legally be reduced further or eliminated altogether. There are loopholes and tax shelters galore (many of them enumerated, for instance, in the *New York Times* of December 1, 1996), and legislative attempts to eliminate them have only been partly successful. The business executive, for instance, can deduct his two-martini–filet-mignon lunch at a first-class restaurant as a business expense if he uses it—or says he uses it—to discuss business, but the worker cannot deduct his baloney sandwich when he discusses job opportunities or pay scales with another worker. Corporations, to give just one more example, can deduct as a business expense stock options given to their executives (in other words, the right to buy a certain, usually very substantial number of shares of stock in the future at the current price, no matter how high the stock market goes). Labelling this as an "executive performance incentive," they thereby circumvent a 1994 tax law that does not allow businesses to deduct as a business expense more than a million dollars in salaries for their highest-paid officers.

"Taxes," said Supreme Court Justice Oliver Wendel Holmes (1841–1935), "are the price we are paying for (living in) a civilized society." And right he was. But those among us who can afford it most seem least willing to pay that price. Our taxes are less progressive and our people, and especially our well-to-do, are taxed at a lower rate than anywhere else in the industrialized world. No wonder, then, that our government offers the least in services to our people among all the industrialized countries. So the question is this: Do we really want Washington to continue pursuing policies of lowering taxes, especially of the wealthiest among us, at the expense of social services, of widening the gap between the rich and the poor, and of making our tax system even less progressive than it is? Or are we ready to follow the historic path other nations have followed, a path of a tax structure aimed at a more equitable distribution of wealth and income, a more equitable allocation of the burden of taxation, a tax structure that would enable our government to attend more effectively to the needs of our people, a tax structure more reflective of the obligations of government in an advanced civilized society? On that decisions hinges, to a great extent, the structure of our society in the twenty-first century.

Chapter 14

Conclusion: Are You Any Wiser Now That You've Read This Book?

This book was written between 1996 and 1999. By the time you read it, much may have changed: new laws may have been passed, old ones discarded; annual deficits may have increased, decreased, or even for the moment given way to surpluses; rates of unemployment, of inflation, of interest may have moved up or down; numbers, magnitudes, percentages may not be what they were then. But the conclusion reached, the basic principle remains the same: There is a role for our government and a major role at that, a role not restricted merely to the generally recognized governmental functions of the maintenance of law and order and of national defense. Laissez-faire capitalism may claim that the common good is served best by the uninhibited pursuit of self-interest; but the free market, if left alone, has an ear only for private, money-backed, profit-driven wants, and a deaf ear for public needs.

Of course, today's advocates of a more market-oriented economy do not argue for no government; they argue for less governmental involvement in the economy. But, as this book has tried to show, there is a desperate need for a government that intervenes more, not less, to mitigate the inequities of a free market, to rectify the wrongs, to balance the scales, and to minister to the needs of those who have fallen by the wayside in the competitive struggle for a decent life. Pope John Paul II, on his 1998 visit to Cuba, warned of the "savagery of unbridled capitalism" and admonished the Cuban people not to embrace the "blind market forces" that lead to a society where "the rich grow ever wealthier, while the poor grow ever poorer"—a warning against the excesses of capitalism and the neglect of the poor, repeated in essence during his January 1999 visits to Mexico and to St. Louis, Missouri.

With the profit motive as its driving force capitalism is not, and by its very nature cannot be, as humane, as socially conscious as it is productive. But what good is efficiency, what good is productivity, if it leaves millions behind? The only reason that capitalism can survive, argues the renowned American economist and presidential adviser John Kenneth Galbraith (1908–), is because government humanizes it. "I don't see government as good or bad," he says, "I see it as indispensable. . . . It's not a question of whether government is efficient or inefficient, it's a question of making it better because there is no alternative." And, perhaps, somewhat less categorically, Abraham Lincoln expressed a similar view when he affirmed that "the legitimate object of government is to do for a community of people whatever they need to have done but cannot do so well for themselves."

In his presidential acceptance speech in January 1997, President Clinton said that government is not the problem and government is not the solution. But, as we have seen, there are countless issues in the social domain—be it in regard to the education of the young, health care for the elderly, food and shelter for the homeless, or protection of the environment—that the free market by its very nature cannot address adequately. Contrary to what we are made to believe, in all such areas we need more, not less government, a more humane, a more compassionate government to be sure, a government that pays at least as much attention to human needs as it does to the protection of private property, but a government nevertheless that takes an active hand and intercedes where and whenever necessary.

While the protection of property interests has always ranked high on Washington's priority list, government intervention aimed at correcting social inequities and promoting the public good is not new. It didn't start with Franklin Delano Roosevelt's New Deal, Harry Truman's Fair Deal, and Lyndon B. Johnson's Great Society. It has been prevalent throughout our history, dating back to Andrew Jackson's campaign against the "elitist," Bank of the United States, then the abolition of slavery, the breaking up of monopolies at the time of Woodrow Wilson, the passage of legislation that prohibited child labor and of other laws that provided for financing of public schools. And in more recent years, job-creation measures to combat the depression of the 1930s, the protection of the poor, the elderly, the environment, the struggle for civil rights and for equal rights for women. Incomplete solutions they may be as yet, but necessary nevertheless to pave the way toward a better future.

In a 1977 address to the U.S. Senate, then Senator Hubert Humphrey said that "the moral test of government is how it treats those who are in the dawn of life—the children; those who are in the twilight of life—the aged; and those who are in the shadows of life—the sick, the needy and the handicapped." For half a century, we made at least passing grades on this test: The food stamp program has fed the hungry, social security has offered a better life to the elderly, Medicare and Medicaid have improved the lot of the sick, unemployment compensation has provided an invaluable measure of economic security for those who lost their jobs without any fault of their own. Workers whose health and life were endangered by unsafe working conditions, by faulty equipment, or by chemicals and dust that caused cancer and black-lung disease found protection under government-enforced regulations; consumer protection agencies provided some safeguard to consumers against harmful, useless, or misrepresented products, and our air is cleaner, our water purer, and our environment healthier than it would have been without government action.

But now, since the beginning of the 1980s, much of the slow and patient progress toward a more decent, more public-spirited society has been eroded. These days, we are willing to sacrifice the well-being of millions on the altar of a balanced-budget philosophy that seems less dedicated to financial accountability (to wit, recent tax cuts for the wealthy) than to the crippling of longstanding social programs and the transfer of wealth and income from the poorer to the upper classes. Senator Paul Wellstone (D-MN) described so well how we are moving backward, toward a more stratified America, "one with mounting access to the things that make life richer, the other caught in a constant struggle to make ends meet; one able to purchase the security of gated communities and private schools, the other beset by the dangers of a decaying social fabric; one swiftly navigating the information superhighway, the other lacking the rudimentary skills needed to navigate an ever more complex society; one enriched by a rising stock market, the other at the uncertain mercies of the job market." Indeed, the bridge to the twenty-first century starts looking more and more like a dirt road back to the nineteenth century.

While this book has tried to dispel some widely held myths, it does not claim to have found answers to all the economic and social problems that ail us. But, if it has shown the reader a different road to the future, a road more geared toward the public good than toward the benefit of the few, if it motivates the reader to question every conventional wisdom, no matter how loudly proclaimed, how often repeated, and how widely accepted, and if it prompts the reader to examine carefully all current and proposed government policies—always with the public good first and foremost in mind—then it will have fulfilled its purpose.

For Further Reading

This selected bibliography consists of recently published works that focus on the role of government in each of the social areas covered in this book. The abbreviations after each entry refer to the topics and chapter numbers in this book:

BA = Balancing Budget, Ch. 6; BB = Boom and Bust (Business Cycles), Ch. 3; CA = Capitalism (Theory and Practice), Ch. 1; CE = Correct Economic Policy, Ch. 2; CO = Conclusion, Ch. 14; DW = Distribution of Wealth and Income, Ch. 4; ED = Education, Ch. 11; EN = Environment, Ch. 12; HE = Health Care, Ch. 10; IU = Inflation versus Unemployment, Ch. 5; ND = National Debt, Ch. 7; SS = Social Security, Ch. 8; TX = Taxation, Ch. 13; WE = Welfare, Ch. 9.

Andrews, Charles. *Profit Fever: The Drive to Corporatize Health Care and How to Stop It.* Monroe, ME: Common Courage Press, 1995. HE
Bane, Mary Jo and David T. Ellwood. *Welfare Realities: From Rhetoric to Reform.* Cambridge, MA: Harvard University Press, 1996. WE
Bartlett, Donald L. and James B. Steele. *American: Who Stole the Dream.* Kansas City, MO: Andrews and McMeel, 1996. DW
Beard, Sam. *Restoring Hope in America: The Social Security Solution.* San Francisco: Institute for Comparative Studies, 1996. SS
Benavie, Arthur. *Deficit Hysteria: A Common Sense Look at America's Rush to Balance the Budget.* Westport, CT: Praeger, 1998. BA, ND
Block, Fred et al. *The Mean Season: The Attack on the Welfare State.* New York: Random House, 1987. WE
Borman, Kathryn M. et al. *Implementing Educational Reform: Sociological Perspectives on Educational Policy.* Norwood, NJ: Ablex Publishing, 1996. ED

Boskin, Michael J., ed. *Frontiers of Tax Reform*. Stanford, CA: Stanford University Press, 1996. TX

Bowles, Samuel et al. *After the Waste Land: A Democratic Economics for the Year 2000*. Armonk, NY: M. E. Sharpe, 1990. CA, DW, BB, CO

Burton, C. Emory. *The Poverty Debate: Politics and the Poor in America*. Westport, CT: Greenwood Press, 1992. DW

Cavanaugh, Francis X. *The Truth about the National Debt*. Boston: Harvard Business School Press, 1996. ND, BB

Cheal, David. *New Poverty: Families in Postmodern Society*. Westport, CT: Greenwood Press, 1996. CA, DW, CO

Chinn, Carl. *Poverty amidst Prosperity*. New York: Saint Martin's Press, 1995. DW

Clinchy, Evans, ed. *Transforming Public Education: A New Course for America's Future*. New York: Columbia University Press, 1997. ED

Costa, L. Dora. *The Evolution of Retirement: An American Economic History, 1880–1990*. Chicago: University of Chicago Press, 1998. SS, WE

Cundiff, David and Mary Ellen McCarthy. *The Right Medicines: How to Make Health Care Reform Work Today*. Totowa, NJ: Humana Press, 1994. HE

Daniels, Mark R., ed. *Medicaid Reform and the American States: Case Studies on the Politics of Managed Care*. Westport, CT: Auburn House, 1998. HE

Darby, Michael R. *Reducing Poverty in America: Views and Approaches*. Thousand Oaks, CA: Sage Publications, 1996. DW, IU, WE, ED

Dixon, John E. and Robert P. Scheurell. *Social Security Programs: A Cross-Cultural Comparative Perspective*. Westport, CT: Greenwood Press, 1995. SS

Dowd, Douglas. *Against the Conventional Wisdom: A Primer for Current Economic Controversies and Proposals*. Boulder, CO: Westview Press, 1997. CA, IU, DW, SS, WE, HE, EN, CO

Dowie, Mark. *Losing Ground: American Environmentalism at the Close of the Twentieth Century*. Cambridge, MA: MIT Press, 1995. EN

Eisner, Robert. *Social Security: More Not Less*. New York: Twentieth Century Fund Press, 1998. SS

Elster, Jon and Karl Ove Moene. *Alternatives to Capitalism*. New York: Cambridge University Press, 1993. CA, CO

Epstein, William M. *Welfare in America: How Social Science Fails the Poor*. Madison, WI: University of Wisconsin Press, 1997. WE, DW

Evans, Gary R. *Red Ink: The Budget, Deficit and Debt of the U.S. Government*. San Diego, CA: Academic Press, 1997. BA, ND

Finnegan, William. *Cold New World*. New York: Random House, 1998. DW

Fiorino, Daniel J. *Making Environmental Policy*. Berkeley and Los Angeles: University of California Press, 1995. EN

Fraser, James W. *Reading, Writing and Justice: School Reforms as if Democracy Matters*. Albany, NY: State University of New York Press, 1997. ED

Fuhrman, Susan H. and Jennifer A. O'Day, eds. *Rewards and Reform: Creating Educational Incentives that Work*. San Francisco: Jossey-Bass Publishers, 1996. ED

Galbraith, John Kenneth. *The Good Society*. Boston and New York: Houghton-Mifflin, 1996. CA, DW, CO

Gates, Jeffrey R. *The Ownership Solution: Toward a Shared Capitalism for the Twenty-first Century*. Reading, MA: Addision-Wesley, 1998. DW, CA, CO

Gillette, Michael L. *Launching the War on Poverty*. New York: Twayne Publishers, 1996. DW

Glaser, William A. *Health Insurance in Practice: International Variations in Financing, Benefits, and Problems*. San Francisco: Jossey-Bass Publishers, 1991. HE

Goodwin, Neva R., ed. *As if the Future Mattered: Translating Social and Economic Theory into Human Behavior*. Ann Arbor, MI: University of Michigan Press, 1996. CA, CO

Gordon, John Steele. *Hamilton's Blessing: The Extraordinary Life and Times of Our National Debt*. New York: Walker and Company, 1997. BA, ND

Gramlich, Edward M. *Is It Time to Reform Social Security?* Ann Arbor, MI: University of Michigan Press, 1998. SS

Grant, James. *The Trouble with Prosperity*. New York: Random House, 1996. BB

Gray, Bradford H. *The Profit Motive and Patient Care: The Changing Accountability of Doctors and Hospitals*. Cambridge, MA: Harvard University Press, 1991. HE

Handler, Joel F. *The Poverty of Welfare Reform*. New Haven, CT: Yale University Press, 1995. WE

Hedrick, Max. *Rethinking Health Care: Innovation and Change in America*. Boulder, CO: Westview Press, 1998. HE

Heilbroner, Robert and Peter Bernstein. *The Debt and the Deficit: False Alarms/Real Possibilities*. New York: W. W. Norton, 1989. BA, ND

Heirich, Max. *Rethinking Health Care: Innovation and Change in America*. Boulder, CO: Westview Press, 1998. HE

Herman, Edward S. *Triumph of the Market*. Boston: South End Press, 1995. CA, IU, EN

Higgins, Benjamin. *Employment Without Inflation*. New Brunswick, NJ: Transaction Publishers, 1998. BB, IU

Holloway, Susan D. et al. *Through My Own Eyes: Single Mothers and the Cultures of Poverty*. Cambridge, MA: Harvard University Press, 1997. DW, WE

Howe, Harold II. *Thinking about Our Kids*. New York: The Free Press, 1993. ED

Imig, Douglas R. *Poverty and Power: The Political Representation of Poor Americans*. Lincoln, NE: University of Nebraska Press, 1996. DW

Jargowski, Paul A. and Rudolf Steiner. *Poverty and Place: Ghettos, Barrios, and the American City*. New York: Russell Sage Foundation, 1996. DW

Jennings, Edward T. and Neal S. Zank, eds. *Welfare System Reform: Coordinating Federal, State, and Local Public Assistance Programs*. Westport, CT: Greenwood Press, 1993. WE

Jones, Stanley R. and Marion Ein Lewin. *Improving the Medicare Market: Adding Choice and Protections*. Washington, DC: National Academy Press, 1996. HE

Kelso, William A. *Poverty and the Underclass: Changing Perceptions of the Poor in America*. New York: New York University Press, 1994. DW, WE

Kempton, Willett et al. *Environmental Values in American Culture*. Cambridge, MA: MIT Press, 1995. EN

Kingfisher, Catherine Pélissier. *Women in the American Welfare Trap*. Philadelphia: University of Pennsylvania Press, 1996. DW, WE

Kingson, Eric R. and Edward D. Berkowitz. *Social Security and Medicare: A Policy Primer*. Westport, CT: Auburn House, 1993. SS, HE

Konner, Melvin. *Medicine at the Crossroads*. New York: Pantheon Books, 1993. HE

Kreml, William P. *America's Middle Class: From Subsidy to Abandonment*. Durham, NC: Carolina Academic Press, 1997. CA, CO, DW

Kronenwetter, Michael. *Welfare State America: Safety Net or Social Contract?* Danbury, CT: Franklin Watts, 1993. WE

Kronfeld, Jennie Jacobs. *The Changing Federal Role in U.S. Health Care Policy*. Westport, CT: Praeger, 1997. HE

Kuttner, Robert. *Everything for Sale: The Virtues and Limits of Markets*. New York: Alfred A. Knopf, 1997. CA, CO

Lindsey, Duncan. *The Welfare of Children*. New York: Oxford University Press, 1994. DW, WE

Mansfield, Edwin. *Leading Economic Controversies of 1998*. 4th ed. New York: W. W. Norton, 1998. CA, SS, TX, ED, CO

Michelman, Irving S. *The Moral Limits of Capitalism*. Brookfield, VT: Ashgate Publishing, 1994. CA, CO, IU

Mink, Gwendolyn. *Welfare's End*. Ithaca, NY: Cornell University Press, 1998. WE

Moon, Marilyn. *Medicare Now and in the Future*. 2nd ed. Washington, DC: The Urban Institute Press, 1996. HE

Moore, Thomas S. *The Disposable Work Force: Worker Displacement and Employment Instability in America*. Hawthorne, NY: Walter de Gruyter, 1996. IU

Morgan, Iwan W. *Deficit Government: Taxing and Spending in Modern America*. Chicago: Ivan R. Dee, 1995. BA, ND, TX

New York Times. *Capitalism: The Downsizing of America*. New York: New York Times Company, 1996. DW, IU

Noble, Charles. *Welfare as We Knew It: A Political History of the American Welfare State*. New York: Oxford University Press, 1997. WE

Noll, James William and Jennifer A. O'Day, eds. *Taking Sides: Clashing Views on Controversial Educational Issues*. Guilford, CT: The Dushkin Publishing Group, 1993. ED

Norris, Donald F. and Lyke Thompson. *The Politics of Welfare Reform*. Thousand Oaks, CA: Sage Publications, 1995. WE

O'Brien, Raymond C. and Michael T. Flannery. *Long-Term Care: Federal, State, and Private Options for the Future*. New York: Haworth Press, 1997. HE

Panis, Constantijn W. A. and Lee A. Lillard. *Social Security, Adequacy, Reforms*. Santa Monica, CA: Rand, 1996. SS

Paris, David C. *Ideology and Educational Reform: Themes and Theories in Public Education*. Boulder, CO: Westview Press, 1995. ED

Rank, Mark Robert. *Living on the Edge: The Realities of Welfare in America*. New York: Columbia University Press, 1994. WE

Rényi, Judith. *Going Public Schooling for a Diverse Democracy*. New York: The New Press, 1993. ED

Research and Policy Committee of the Committee for Economic Development. *Fixing Social Security*. New York: Committee for Economic Development (CED), 1997. SS

Roemer, Milton I. *National Health Systems of the World*. 2 vols. New York: Oxford University Press, 1993. HE

Rosa, Jean-Jacques et al., eds. *Advances in Health Economics and Health Services Research: Comparative Health Systems: The Future of National Health Care Systems and Economic Analysis*. Greenwich, CT: JAI Press, 1990. HE

Rose, Nancy E. *Workfare or Fair Work: Women, Welfare and Govenrment Work Programs*. New Brunswick, NJ: Rutgers University Press, 1995. WE, DW

Rosenthal, Marilynn M. and Max Heirich. *Health Policy: Understanding Our Choices from National Reform to Market Forces*. Boulder, CO: Westview Press, 1998. HE

Ross, Jean-Jaques et al., eds. *Advances in Health Economics and Health Services Research: Comparative Health Systems: The Future of National Health Care Systems and Economic Analysis*. Greenwich, CT: JAI Press, 1990. HE

Shaviro, Daniel. *Do Deficits Matter?* Chicago: University of Chicago Press, 1997. BA, ND

Silk, Leonard and Mark Silk et al. *Making Capitalism Work*. New York: Twentieth Century Fund, 1996. CA, CO

Sklar, Holly. *Chaos or Community*. Boston: South End Press, 1995. DW, IU

Sklar, Holly. *Jobs, Income and Work: Ruinous Trends, Urgent Alternatives*. Philadelphia: American Friends Service Committee, 1995. IU, SS, WE, HE, EN

Smith, David G. *Paying for Medicare: The Politics of Reform*. New York: Aldine de Gruyter, 1992. HE

Solow, Robert M. et al. *Inflation, Unemployment and Monetary Policy*. Cambridge, MA: MIT Press, 1998. IU

Spreding, C. J., ed. *National Health Care*. Commack, NY: Nova Science Publishers, 1993. HE

Steinmo, Sven. *Taxation and Democracy: Swedish, British and American Approaches to Financing the Modern States*. New Haven, CT: Yale University Press, 1993. TX

Sultz, Harry A. and Kristina M. Young. *Health Care USA: Understanding Its Organization and Delivery*. Gaithersburg, MD: Aspen Publishers, 1997. HE

Swartz, Thomas R. and Frank Bonello. *Taking Sides: Clashing Views on Controversial Economic Issues*. Guilford, CT: Dushkin/McGraw-Hill, 1998. CA, CO

Swartz, Thomas R. and Kathleen Mass Weigert, eds. *America's Working Poor*. Notre Dame, IN: University of Notre Dame Press, 1995. DW, IU

Timmer, Doug A. et al. *Paths to Homelessness: Extreme Poverty and the Urban Housing Crises*. Boulder, CO: Westview Press, 1994. BB, DW, WE

Toch, Thomas. *In the Name of Excellence: The Struggle to Reform the Nation's Schools, Why It's Failing, and What Should be Done*. New York: Oxford University Press, 1991. ED

Turgeon, Lynn. *The Search for Economics as a Science* (An annotated bibliography). Lanham, MD: The Scarecrow Press, 1996. CA, CO

Vatter, Harold and John F. Walker. *The Inevitability of Government Growth*. New York: Columbia University Press, 1990. BA, BB, ND

Weissman, Joel S. and Arnold M. Epstein. *Falling through the Safety Net: Insurance Status and Access to Health Care*. Baltimore, MD: John Hopkins University Press, 1994. HE

Werbach, Adam. *Act Now, Apologize Later*. New York: Cliff Street Books, 1997. EN

Westerfield, Donald L. *National Health Care: Law, Policy, Strategy*. Westport, CT: Praeger, 1993. HE

Wilber, Charles K. and Kenneth P. Jameson. *Beyond Reagonomics: A Further Inquiry in the Poverty of Economics.* Notre Dame, IN: University of Notre Dame Press, 1990. CA, BB, CO

Wollman, William and Anne Colamosca. *The Judas Economy: The Triumph of Capital and the Betrayal of Work.* Reading, MA: Addison-Wesley Longman, 1997. CA, DW, ED, SS, HE, CO

Worth, Richard. *Poverty.* San Diego, CA: Lucent Books, 1997. DW

Yates, Michael D. *Longer Hours, Fewer Jobs.* New York: Monthly Review Press, 1994. CA, DW, IU

Zucchino, David. *Myth of the Welfare Queen.* New York: Scribner, 1997. DW, WE

Index

About the Author

HARRY G. SHAFFER is Professor Emeritus of Economics at the University of Kansas. His ten published books include *The Soviet Treatment of Jews* (1974), *Women in the Two Germanies: A Comparison of Socialist and Non-Socialist Society* (1981), and *The Soviet System in Theory and Practice: Selected Western and Soviet Views* (1984).

ISBN 0-275-96578-3

90000>

HARDCOVER BAR CODE